MIDNIGHT RAMBLINGS

GEORGANNE ALDRICH

PAGE PUBLISHING
Conneaut Lake, PA

First originally published by Page Publishing 2022

ISBN 979-8-88654-036-9 (pbk)
ISBN 979-8-88654-200-4 (hc)
ISBN 979-8-88654-053-6 (digital)

Printed in the United States of America

Midnight Ramblings

I owe the idea of writing this book to the endless encouragement
of a sex therapist, my granddaughter Nicoletta Heidegger.

And I would like to thank my daughter, Jami Morse
Heidegger, who encouraged me all the way. Maggie Ribeiro
who helped me believe that writing this book was worthwhile.
Kimberly Ford's insights and encouragements were so
important and JuliAnne DeChaine's help and hard work
made this book a reality. And I must thank my partner,
Robert Leroy, who supported me every step of the way.

Cover collage by
Georganne Aldrich Heller

TABLE OF CONTENTS

Don't Ask What I Had to Do

I was turning eighty-nine. How could that be?

I felt like Forty, except for a boot on my foot after ankle surgery.

Eight-nine, of course, is nothing like turning ninety.

Ask my new live-in beau. He's an outdoors man. We met four years ago and are living together in Beverly Hills and the West Village. He loves camping and the great outdoors. He tells me stories of stalking through the woods with his gun for protection. Of course, he's eighty-four now. In his head, this is still his life.

When we first met, he asked if I loved the outdoors and the woods.

"Of course I do. Whenever the weather's nice I leave the Village and go all the way uptown to walk in Central Park."

Bob laughed like I was telling a joke, which of course I was not.

Bob is tall and attractive. He's gentle, caring and a great chef and since I only knew the culinary art of Takeout or Asking Cook What's for Dinner, I was excited with the idea of a man who loves a sauté pan.

But back to my birthday. My possible husband-number-seven told me he'd brought me something I would love and "go on loving. Not just for the day. You'll love it all year."

It wouldn't be a facelift, which I would have loved, because that lasts even longer than a year.

A dog? But I think not. Bob knows he'd be the one to walk it.

I'd already received several orchids. Maybe it was a year's worth of massages with my wonderful Japanese masseur who brings flowers from the Wall Street Market whenever he comes.

Smiling, he said, "Oh, stop guessing." Bob was all too pleased with himself. Which was charming in its own right.

That night I went to sleep dreaming how great I would look should it be a facelift. Along with that, I would treat myself to a professional makeup session before the Arts Gala and of course I'd have to buy Bob a new tuxedo as he came with only stalking boots and khaki vests with far too many pockets.

You know life after eighty-nine can be an adventure. You just have to gear yourself toward being positive at all times. Never let your hair grow grey. Agree to meet any new suitor. Doesn't hurt to live half the time in California.

Finally: it was my birthday morning. Bob, in khaki pants with fewer pockets than the vests in the closet, was so anxious he said I must get dressed and head outside right away to see my gift.

Outside?

I dressed and came out as quickly as my ankle-boot would allow. I looked up and down the street but saw nothing special.

Bob came close, took my arm. "Well. Here it is!"

Here's *what*?

He stepped across the sidewalk and curb to the street. He flung open the door of a tall silver van-like vehicle. "Hop in!"

"Hop in" took five minutes with my boot and the van's shallow rubberized steps and the swivel seat blocking the way.

"Isn't it wonderful?" He peered up from the sidewalk to where I stood stooped and squeezed between a narrow couch and a glossy faux-wood wall. "You love a Mercedes, Georanne! This is the new size. So compact. You have everything: microwave, big TV, solar panels. An *actual bathroom*. Those two couches make up into beds!

If you weighed under 100 pounds.

My shock was so great I didn't know how to respond.

You should know that I'm somewhat claustrophobic. Bob might not have. Immediately, there was no air inside the vehicle. "I feel," I said, "closed in."

"Not to worry," said he. "Customization! We'll have more windows installed."

But. But. "My—" I was at a loss. "My clothes…"

Bob climbed aboard—also stooped, also squeezed—and the walls moved in. He tapped on the narrow panel. "Closet!" He pointed to the bottom portion of the "closet." "Even a large drawer right there. Oh, you're going to love this. Who cares about the pandemic? We can go anywhere. We have all we will need right here."

Everything? My medications would take both "closet" and "drawer." My espresso machine? My make-up mirror? My cosmetics would need a small trailer just for themselves. Whatever was I going to do?

Bob took my hand. "Please get ready. I've reserved us a whole weekend up at the Malibu RV park. *Great* view of the ocean."

Oh my Lord. What if any of my Malibu friends saw me in this van. Julia or Mystica or anyone else in the Colony.

Oblivious, he threw open a tiny refrigerator stocked with a dozen eggs, my favorite lasagna and some fruit yogurt. He told me the TV would be great once it was hooked up and the air-conditioning was very effective, but we needed a different connection if we wanted heat. Even on this warm August morning, California sun bright through the tinted window, I was chilly.

"It'll be—" Bob helped me down and toward the house to pack. "It will be the best."

*

Large-brim hat, sunblock, Tylenol, Advil, vitamins, sandals, whistle, phone, phone charger, two pair of sunglasses, deck of cards, shower cap and many medications. One for motion sickness.

After an hour we arrived at Malibu Beach Recreational Vehicle Park where we were assigned spot #42. After pulling in, overlooking the ocean, Bob sat with hands on the wheel. "Tell me how peaceful this is."

Was he referring to the hippies next door in #43 with their ancient converted school bus, their three dogs and the two-year-old who was, even then, screaming? I looked out my window to where the older children were having fun trying to make the baby play ball. She was too small and screamed and screamed.

I turned back to find Bob gone. Making my way between our seats into the back, I saw through the open side-door a joyous Bob putting up the awning that extended out to within feet of the hippies' smoldering hibachi. Under the awning were two folding chairs. So we could enjoy the view even from the outside.

I had just sunk to the "couch," wondering what could be making the noise coming from the neighbors on the *other* side when an enormous German Shepherd bounded into the van. I screamed. Bob was happily working on the awning and my cries might have been lost with the baby's or the other-side neighbor's loud music. Either way, he didn't hear. I screamed loudly enough, though, that I terrified the dog who went leaping out, which brought Bob running.

"What's wrong what's wrong?"

Oh nothing, I was almost attacked by the neighbor's dog, which my granddaughter Nicoletta Heidegger than the next adventure, which was Bob mistakenly opening the bathroom door in the side of the van only to have a couple from the beach path wave to where I was sitting on the toilet in full view.

"I'm so sorry, G." He said after the bathroom incident. "You'll get used to all this. You'll see. It's part of the adventure!"

The adventure I was looking forward to was the weekend being over. Happily, it was starting to get dark.

On separate, tiny folding tables we ate the lasagne which was cold because the stove wasn't connected. Bob didn't mind. "Part of the adventure!"

Because we were parked at an incline, his food kept slipping off the little table but Bob just laughed and laughed. He winked at me and said, "Almost time to experience your first night sleeping in the ol' land yacht."

An experience it was. The twin beds were so narrow that if I turned over, I would be on the floor. I snugged as close to the wall as possible but again, that incline. I spent the night capturing my blanket from the floor and rolling to the edge of my bed and almost falling out.

Somehow the hours passed. On Saturday, the baby mostly stopped crying and we had no more visits from the German Shepherd. Despite having discovered—when we were back at home—a second small drawer marked "wardrobe," I couldn't even think of changing for "dinner" that evening after the five-minute's walk we took—remember, plastic boot—on the cliff-side path. Finally, it was Sunday.

Bob drove while I bumped around on the narrow couch that had been my "bed" the night before. I needed a small remove from my beloved—to think. I also needed a moment for research on my phone. How best to word a speech that said, "Thank you for your desire to make this a perfect birthday, but I think we have to talk."

Finally, Bob stood on the Beverly Hills sidewalk I never knew I could miss so dearly. He raised a gentlemanly hand to assist me down the rubber steps and I blurted, "We need to sell this camper immediately. I am not cut out for van vacations."

He looked like a little boy after someone had stolen his truck. "You don't think you'll grow to love camping and traveling in our beautiful RV?"

"No, darling, I just don't! You're so wonderful. You are. But, Bob, darling. Think about it."

I was nothing, after all, if not a woman who had run a public relations firm, launched a successful New York jazz club and helped found Los Angeles's fabled Ma Maison. I had produced innumerable international plays and had run a clothing company. At eighty-nine, I sat on three different non-profit boards. I had negotiated six divorces in such a way that I owned, outright, a home in Greenwich Village as well as the charming five-bedroom Beverly Hills bungalow with the walk-in closet and dressing room that I had *never fully appreciated till now.*

There on the step I stood slightly over him. "Bob. Darling. Listen for a moment. I have some very good news. We are in the middle of a once-in-a-century global pandemic. No one could have predicted that the market for recreational vehicles would balloon the way it has. I can tell you right now, my love, that with the profit we will make from the sale of this very thoughtful birthday gift, we can stay in the most luxurious new resort in Tulum. You can scuba dive, bob, every single day."

Now. Don't ask what I had to do to fully convince my man that the sale would be the best idea. I'll leave that to your imagination.

But ultimately, Bob—like me—has a head for business. Today he enjoys the pleasure of knowing he made a great deal selling the van at a significant profit, after "enjoying" it for a weekend.

And I can tell you, Bob made an even greater deal having me as his mate.

THE VOYAGE

It was a foggy morning. At six the air felt heavy and not welcoming. It was a good day for a VOYAGE.

*

Her friend had told her, "Sure you can write. I know you can. Just talking to you is like reading a novel."

"But where to start?"

"Easy. Just write about a voyage."

I put the word in front of me. And it began:

*

My aunt in her stateroom embarking on another glamorous ocean crossing. This time, the *Queen Mary*.

Was it the *Queen*? Or do I think that because she always told us she was one, and demanded to be treated in that royal fashion?

Perhaps the most royal thing about her was that she always had something snide to say:

"Why are you dressed like that? Is the circus in town?"

Or:

"The men you choose, you'll surely never go on a trip like this."

Money never became her. It simply wasn't something she needed to understand. The crossing and the queenliness, yes, that she understood. But money simply needn't enter into a life with maids who took care of everything. Her husband was with her checking reservations, calling for cars.

To my young eyes she was all anyone would ever dream to be.

She had the most perfect marriage—her husband hadn't dared to voice a disagreement with her on any issue for thirty years. She had the "best," most important friends, who lived close to her in Palm Beach. She had the most beautiful legs I had ever seen along with a figure to die for, fashion-magazine taste and the credit accounts to indulge it.

She, my mother's only sister, lived next door to us no matter where we moved. Both in New York and in Palm Beach. Mother felt it was imperative that her sister's haughty, arrogant, controlling ways dominated our household at all times. Mother? She was incapable of functioning alone. It was my aunt who spoke for her. This aunt was part of it. Part of the heavy weather I experienced when my childhood memories were being made, moving by me like thunderclouds.

When I was very young, I would stand in the doorway of her bathroom to see all the beauty products and make-up she applied. The doorway led to the world of the most sophisticated people.

I would never be one of them. Because, according to Haughty Auntie, my chances were *slim*.

Was all of this—applying lipstick, all the exciting hair preparations—was this what it meant to be a grown up?

My chances to be like her were almost nil, so I wouldn't need the vials and brushes and tubes. There was only the very slimmest of chances that I would even own scented lotions, never perfume from Paris.

Through the doorway I got a glimpse of silks of the best quality, beautiful evening dresses. There were steamer trunks and the most *divine* friends and designer sportswear.

But my childish question? Even then?

Where was the laughter?

*

Little did I realize that my own voyage, the one that would soon begin, would also lack laughter and happiness.

I, too, was about to take a trip. It would be a long voyage, many years' duration. I would have only one destination: survival!

My voyage would be out of misery, incest, loneliness; out of beatings and hatred.

No clinking glasses. Never the scents of wealth or of cocktail pianos.

*

From age eight, I sought the roaring of a subway train, again and again. I would sit alone on these long escapes, huddled in a corner hoping not to be discovered. I was in search of any other family, any other person who might take me in. I searched for any place other than my home. With the screech and slam of each stop, my youth ebbed away.

But there was also triumph.

These forays brought the joy of escape. I would not be the total failure Madame Auntie predicted. I wasn't a total failure at this. I had managed to run away! Again! True, there was the inevitable fear of being found and brought back home again.

And again. And then again. Auntie was right. I was not a success. Not in the camouflage of grays and blues and blacks meant to disguise me from policemen who looked for little girls who ran away. It was their sworn duty to bring little girls back home.

It never seemed their duty to find out why a little girl might have left in the first place.

Auntie's journeys involved farewell parties.

Mine, unlike hers, was no voyage of joy or laughter. Mine led away from the nightly screams of my mother and my stepfather, people who sought to destroy each other but couldn't even succeed at that.

Mine was a voyage to find sanity, which had long before faded with the scent of Auntie's perfume.

Does a Harvard Graduate Have a PhD in Making Love?

She wondered: was it to be he, the Harvard Phi Beta Kappa turned Yale Law bon vivant who lined up his coins in neat stacks of pennies, nickels and quarters on the bureau before coming to bed for what promised to be a well-planned well-ordered sexual escapade?

He surely was good looking.

And had an amazing ability to play jazz piano.

She said: "Can't have sex with you, unless you want to marry me."

Elliot turned from the bureau, mouth slightly open. Only to himself, he said, "Marry?"

He was handsome, but spontaneity was obviously not his strong suit. She bore in mind, of course, that he had been editor of *The Crimson*. He hadn't just graduated Yale Law, but had graduated with honors. She herself had only gone as far as two years at Finch Junior College on the Upper East Side. But survival had been her reason for being, and survival it would be.

It was necessary—this organized man with his organized coins—if the future path was going to lead away from the father who deserted her at birth and the battle she fought to stay afloat in spite of her anxieties. Now, here, lying on the bed in the apartment he shared with no one, she felt great. She was ready for love and security. She knew that her satin nightdress became her in all the right ways. But would he appreciate it? Would it be enough? This needed to be an all-out winning campaign. Would he be the provider? Elliot? The caretaker, companion, lover? Or would there be a next man—her beauty mostly felt like assurance—if this one bolted?

Elliot wondered if he had slung his suit-coat onto the chair in the entryway or if he had—in his eagerness to have this beauty—forgotten it somewhere. His wallet was on the night table, right there next to his apartment keys. First this was a relief, but the wallet and apartment keys meant that the suit-coat, for a second, was even more a mystery. He said, "Unless we're married? We've only known each other two months."

"I know. But I need your decision. We really are perfect together. You said it yourself."

Always looking for a safety net. Honestly, with her history, how could she not? Not love necessarily, or passion. To her it was a reasonable demand: no sex unless she had a proposal. What she needed to use was her beauty and sense of humor. And her intelligence.

After all, everything about him was so *planned.* Suits with tailored vests that flattered his tall body, the gorgeous briefcase he carried to the District Attorney's office with gleaming initials and that polished clasp. How was it that his lovely dark hair never blew across his face in the wind? And where had it come from, the patrician accent? He was Long Island City. It suited him, though, this brilliant, methodical, not terribly emotional new suitor whose knowledge of all things literary and philosophical just might end up being everything she would need.

Never would she say that it was mostly just a roof, not a mad sex life, that she was looking for. She needed a roof that she hoped would never leak and the kind of man who, when the wind really started blowing, didn't even ask before slinging his coat over her shoulders.

The safety net could include friendship, love even. Sure. Good conversation on good days and long shared evenings of *Casablanca* and *Gone with the Wind.*

The net and the roof and the coat around the shoulders, though, all came with the miserable freezing false pleasure she had to play-act, the trial that was, for her, the most dreadful, most idiotic of all events: the Harvard-Yale game. Next weekend.

He had graduated so many years before but still, he knew every-one. It simply could not be this important, that Harvard win. And always, always it was freezing, freezing cold.

She did, though, manage to earn the admiration of the *Crimson* cartoonist whom she met during intermission. Intermission? Half-time. The cartoonist didn't have any use for football either. He had to draw something for the paper.

Many years and one husband later, he was to be her lover.

On that cold, cold afternoon in early September, four months after her wedding to Elliot, she wouldn't have been entirely surprised about the cartoonist, but the two of them didn't *know*. No one in the stadium could.

From just this brief meeting the man would become not only her lover but her frequent rescuer, years later when he visited California, where she would eventually settle, after decades, with a different hus-band. The thing that might have surprised the cartoonist way back then was that in California he would learn the incredible strength of scream therapy and teach it to her.

But on the evening before the game, before the cartoonist, before the wedding when she lay in her nightdress on his bed, Mr. Elliot Good-Enough, Esq. was, in spite of himself, falling for her beauty and her helpless ways.

He knew she wasn't the type of gal he needed. He knew it, but also, he didn't know it. She was a girl who thought Nietzsche was a hand cream. She had said aloud that she thought Yeats and Shelly were pretty boring. She once said, "All you do is read those old books," and he thought she was teasing, or flirting. He had been sure that she was impressed, or intimidated.

Yet there *were* moments when she believed that his knowledge of all things literary and philosophical was everything she wanted. It seemed like the most important thing in the world, his knowledge, but mostly she couldn't figure why he wouldn't prefer skiing or the couples' tango class she had to sign up for alone.

How could she have known that one day in the not-too-dis-tant future her life would change again? She would forsake any kind of nightdress or lingerie. Silk slips and satin nightdresses utterly left behind. She couldn't know that she would run off to Woodstock where everyone was smoking pot and where she would dress like a hippie. She would grow her blond hair long. Temporarily, she would attempt to solve her lifelong loneliness with "group living."

But now, lying on Elliot's bed she was easily convinced that this burnished-leather New England world was just what she desired.

After all, soon, there would be no safety in nights spent in Harlem jazz clubs then going home alone. There would be no roof over her head after those evenings dating an Irish Catholic policemen's son, funny and handsome as he was.

For now, at the football game, four months after her wedding day, Miss Trying Hard sat in the Connecticut stadium. She sat smiling broadly, in a way that was believable because somewhere deep inside herself she understood that in years to come there would be the cartoonist; there would be California. There would be many lives for her.

In the final, final minutes, Harvard—Elliot's true school, his alma mater—lost. The players had done something terrible that she could not understand. They had done something awful, unforgivable. Around her everyone was glum. They were demoralized. It was a calamity.

And though she was so cold, freezing even, she was all right. Because she was not alone. He, for now, was hers.

A Day in the Country: Part One

Only a little girl, she settled comfortably in the backseat of the limousine. They had a special smell, limousines, which—as she grew up—she would associate with money and men in beautifully tailored suits. These were smells that would evoke memories of nights spent driving to fancy restaurants.

But for now, it was only a fun smell. She was going to visit her daddy for the first time in a faraway place called the country. She wondered if the doormen there said, "And how are you, young lady?"

But then, it was called "the country." She had never been before.

But then, that wasn't really true.

Nanny took her to the country with the big rocks to climb called Central Park where sometimes she got ice cream from the man with the bright yellow cart. But only on special days. Days when Nanny didn't have to say, "Button up!" as she pulled her fur hood over her ears, Nanny saying, "Children catch their death on days like this."

Today, the sun was shining. She was going, all by herself, to that Faraway Place. "Connecticut." Nanny said it was the *real* country.

She hoped Daddy's building would be nothing like that office of his with that big desk where he cleared his throat and cut the tips off cigars while people came in to ask questions. The prettiest of these ladies were called models, but they weren't allowed to say a single word.

It was always another woman, not quite as pretty, who leaned down to the little girl to whisper, "Your daddy is such a famous coo-too-ri-EH." It sounded so special, so beautiful. When she tried to say it everyone laughed though her daddy didn't pay her any attention at all.

He did say, "You'll come to the country." So maybe he liked her even if he said she wasn't such a nice girl. He told her nice girls didn't sit cross their legs. They certainly didn't have their panties show.

But the country! It would be the *best* of times.

The man behind the wheel wore shiny black. He said, "Just speak up, little girl. That's what I'm here for."

He sounded nice but spoke funny. Maybe he lived in a different farther-away country. He looked a lot like a man who came to fix the stove who gave her a shiny red hard-candy and said, "That's for you, because you're such a polite little girl."

It wasn't Mommy who taught her to be polite. She rarely saw Mommy. Nanny was supposed to tell her if she wasn't polite. That was the most important thing to remember when she got to the country, because sometimes she forgot to say thank you or please.

Goodness, she'd never seen trees so big, and with such golden leaves! She could ask Mr. Shiny-Cap to get out and gather some of the leaves—so many colors—on the ground so she could bring them home, but she knew better than to ask. Besides, then it would take longer to get there.

Someone else, another day, not in her father's office, said, "Your Daddy? He's a *big* man, very big. That's verrrry important."

But she didn't know what the person meant, because her father looked the same size as every other man, though he did smell of something lovely.

The toe of one of her shoes looked like something had fallen on it. She could only hope that no one would notice. And just like the man who came to fix the stove and who brought her a candy, Mr. Shiny-Cap stopped at a red traffic light that was not on a pole but hung from a wire over the middle of the road. The lollipop Mr. Shiny handed her was green. She didn't like green, but she was getting hungry.

Could this be the country right outside her limousine window?

It was nice. Colorful.

But she missed the tall buildings and garbage trucks, babies being pushed in carriages and grown-ups walking dogs. Or maybe the same things happen in the country but everyone here was still asleep.

She decided, although she herself had been up for hours, that it must have been very early in the morning. No one else in Connecticut was awake.

A Day in the Country: Part Two

The car turned onto what Mr. Shiny-Cap said was Main Street.

Never had she seen a place so lovely: big houses like in storybooks with white fences and the most beautiful flowers.

There was a church and some little stores. She wished she could get out and see if they had things she would like, paper dolls or jacks. She wondered if one of the places sold ice-cream sandwiches. She loved changing paper dolls' dresses. But like the models at Daddy's office, dolls weren't allowed to talk.

Though none of that mattered. Her daddy would have a car and be happy to bring her to these stores again.

Suddenly they were pulling into a driveway that made a lot of noise because it was filled with pebbles. Christmas trees lined the driveway, but with no shiny balls or pretty ornaments. The trees themselves were stuck into the ground. A dog was barking. She thought: I have never been so happy.

She climbed out of the car quickly but was very careful not to forget her little bag. Mr. Shiny-Cap might never return. She stood on tiptoes to ring the doorbell and heard chimes. Daddy opened the door. He was dressed in a costume with tan pants that ended at his knees and shiny black boots. The blond lady standing beside him wore the same costume, her white blouse with a ruffle. The lady didn't smile.

Her father pointed to the lady and said, "This is Wynne." He patted the little girl on the head. "Wynne and I are exercising the horses. It's been raining for days. We've got to get going. You stay right here, right by the fire with Donnie till we get back."

She looked beyond the grown-ups. There was no nanny whose name might be Donnie. Her father said, then, as a small golden dog ran near, "Here's my Donnie-girl. You're my Donnie-girl, aren't you. Aren't you."

To the little girl he said, "Donnie likes her head scratched." Then, starting to leave: "We left you a banana and a glass of milk on the table, there, by the fireside."

She wanted to ask them, "Am I really staying here alone?"

But she remembered what her mother had told her: 'No one will like you if you're not polite." She had a sense that asking would be impolite.

And never had she seen a real fire before. This one made the loudest cracking noises and smelled ever so wonderful.

And Donnie loved her right away. They sat by the cozy fire. The girl wondered who the blond lady was and what it could possibly be like to live here with Christmas tress that grew in the ground and fires in fireplaces and the sweetest little dog.

But when it began to get dark and she was still alone, she realized had grown scared. What if she caught her death? No one would find her here. When Nanny said she would be back soon, she came back very quickly with apples and lettuce and sometimes candy and milk and bread. When would her father be back?

Her wonderful new friend Donnie gave her kisses as if to say, "Don't be afraid! We're here together!" Still, she worried she was going to cry.

But the door banged open: Daddy and Miss Blondie.

"Have a nice afternoon, Lydia?" her daddy asked.

"Well, yes. I mean, I did. But I'm awfully glad you're back."

As if he'd just thought of it, he said, "I'll show you your room."

Up a flight of stairs with pretty blue carpet was her room: warm with a great quilt made of many colored patches. She liked to count patches and play games with them. "Your room is just outside of our room," he was saying, "so you won't feel too far away."

She could feel that he was paying attention, so she worked up the courage to ask who Miss Blondie was.

"Why, Wynne's your stepmother." He glanced toward the doorway and down the stairs to where the lady might still be. He said, "She's my wife."

"Maybe a stepmother will have more time than Mommy."

"Doesn't your mother have time for you?"

It was so difficult to know what to say. "She goes to a lot of dress-up parties. Often, she's asleep in the morning when I leave for school. When I get home, Nanny is there. We have milk and crackers and peanut butter sandwiches. She tells me if Mommy had to meet friends or go to a beauty parlor. She's really very busy. Mother."

"Oh," he said, in a way that didn't feel happy.

But she tried hard not to notice because this was her first night in a place called the country and maybe if her father liked her, he would invite her again. Next time he might even take her along to see horses.

But for now, all her father said was that she ought to get ready for dinner.

She didn't know what that meant. She couldn't ask because already he had gone.

But she did think to herself, standing alone in a room that was very pretty and that was supposed to be hers, that she could not remember a single time in her whole life when she felt so very, very hungry.

Evening with Sally

I was almost out of breath from jumping up and down when Fraulein's key turned in the lock.

"Fraulein, Fraulein." I met her in the foyer. "Do you think Mommy will say I can go to Sally's house for dinner on Sunday?"

"Yes, Little Sweetie," as she called me. "I think so."

"But maybe you'd ask her for me?"

Sunday was Fraulein's day off, but couldn't she pick me up after a day of doing what Fraulein did on Sundays and go with me across town in a taxi?

When Fraulein told me Mommy said I could go I spun around three times as I did often and kissed the air. That was my way of saying THANK YOU, GOD! Fraulein said you must always do that when things go well.

Where is God when things go so badly? Oh, don't think of that now. But the time went ever so slowly. Wednesday, Thursday. Would it never be Sunday? I saw Sally in school on Friday and she hugged me and said she would see me at her house soon.

What would I wear? My new velvet party dress? We might play a lot and I might get it dirty and Mommy would be angry. My blue dress with the white sweater. Would that be good?

"Fraulein, what do you think?"

She was busy writing one of those German letters. She didn't look up.

"Fraulein! What do you think?"

She looked up. "What about your blue dress? I think that would be perfect, but I must get this letter in the post."

Who was she writing to in that far off place? Does she tell them about me? Will I never meet him? Or maybe her?

Still only Saturday, but I did a lot of pages in my Shirley Temple coloring book so the time would go faster, and in the afternoon we went to the Park.

Finally! It was Sunday. I wanted to get dressed for Sally's right after breakfast. Somehow the day did go by and now it was time to go. The taxi driver finally announced, "One-twenty-six West End Avenue!" and we were there.

Elevator to the third floor. We rang the bell. When Sally answered, I turned back and the elevator, with Fraulein in it, had gone. For a minute I wanted to run and call, "Fraulein!" but I decided to be a very brave girl.

"Georgie! This is my brother, this is Bobbie."

The dog that jumped on me to say hello must have been Rusty. My first outing by myself. Sally's dad, smoking a big pipe, said, "Hi there Georgie, and welcome to our house."

We sat down to dinner with Sally's mother and father and brother. Can you imagine, Sally doesn't eat with her nanny or the maid on Sundays, but with her mommy and daddy. All of them together.

Her daddy asked me many fun questions and he laughed a lot. Her mommy was short and pretty, and can you believe it, was not even wearing lipstick.

Right after dinner Sally took my hand and we went into her room, which was filled with so many fun things, but things that were all over the place not put away on shelves and in cabinets. I couldn't wait to tell Fraulein as she says we must put all our toys away after we play with them as that's how Mommy wants it.

We played dolls and dress up and coloring and the evening went ever so fast. It seemed like everything had just begun when Sally's daddy came in with a big laugh. "Georgie, your Fraulein's here to pick you up but we wish you could stay longer. We hope you'll be coming back soon."

And wait till you hear this. He leaned down and gave me a hug. Honest. He was not like all the Uncle Mikes that came to take Mommy out. Tears welled in my eyes, but I held them back.

Nanny, by Sally's door said, "Say thank you now, Georgie."

"Thank you very much I had a very nice time." Fraulein and I had practiced that.

"What a polite girl you are," her daddy said. "Maybe you can teach that to Sally." He grinned and laughed and brought me down the hall and to the door where Fraulein was waiting.

At the elevator I said, "Oh, I have so much to tell you! They were so nice to me! We had ice cream with chocolate syrup. Her mommy and daddy sat with us at dinner. Rusty licked my hand but didn't bite and Sally let me play with all her toys."

Fraulein smiled. "That makes me very happy, Little Sweetie. You deserve a fun evening like this many times."

But all the way home I thought, will I ever be asked to come back? Did they really like me? Did I behave like a good girl?

Mommy and her newest Mike were not home yet, so in my room Fraulein got out my favorite pajamas, the ones with the bears on them. She said it was time to say my prayers and turn off the light as tomorrow was a school day.

She left and tears soaked my pillow.

What if they never ask me back? Could it really be true that there are homes where you sit together, play together, and maybe never get spanked? What would it be like to have a daddy who called you sweetie?

What would it be like to have a real dog?

PAYNE WHITNEY

The nurse seemed to have assured herself that the only dangerous weapon I was carrying was the one inside me. The one giving me this ongoing feeling of fear.

"Here. You can use these pajamas. They're soft, comfortable."

Pajamas at three in the afternoon? But yes. That's right. I had brought nothing with me.

"How can I get some clothes and some belongings? Can I use the telephone please?" I needed to call my father. There was some huge mistake. He told me he was taking me to a visit with a psychiatrist. Now, I was a patient in a mental institution.

"Where are my new Italian boots? My dress—the dark green wool? With the antique pin?"

"Oh, we'll return your possessions in due time." The nurse had said her name was Robin. She was softening up a bit, now that she saw I was only pathetic. "No telephones here. Your records show you're fine. Physically. Very healthy. But this is the place you want to be. If you're ever to get well. One day you'll thank your father."

In the strange long room with the white tile floor, with benches and long rows of lockers, there were no other patients. I couldn't begin to tell you why, but being alone, with no other sick people in sight, meant that my hopes for escaping waned with each minute.

"You'll be on the 10th floor tonight. Your own room! Don't pay attention to the flashlight in your face every few hours. That'll just be us wanting to make sure you're not doing anything to harm yourself. We'll give you medicine. To help you relax."

"What about Dr. Regan? When will I meet with him? I—"

"First, of course, we'll need you in the bathtubs. Dr. Regan will see you Monday." But my father said he only brought me here to see a doctor. Now I'm locked in.

Monday. Was that months from now? Years? I felt like crawling under the wooden bench or curling myself into one of the metal lockers until Dr. Regan came and knocked and pulled me out. Any of that old feeling of being trapped in a restaurant or a taxi, that fear felt like nothing compared to this place with no windows, with its white metal and white-painted wood. I was hot. Then cold. I was hot and cold. If I didn't grip them in my lap, my hands shook. I thought of Dr. Regan, of my father. I thought of my doorman and a scream for freedom came to my throat but died there.

I was ushered into my new room. I was away from my own room. It was strange, crossing to the thin-blanket bed, I thought: no one can get me here. It was an entirely new thought. In my new hideaway I could be as scared as I wanted to be. No one expected more.

I picked up the thin towel that Nurse Robin pointed out at the foot of the bed. She led me down a hall and through a door to a room filled with steam, teeming with it. Through nothing but vapor and heat, in the middle of a tiled room, stood two large metal tubs. Sterile. Janet, who was Nurse Robin's assistant, said I should get into this deep metal tub. I knew how. I used the bathtub at home far more than often.

Home. That was days ago. I needed to stop thinking of "home." I was confused. They would surely let me out Monday when they realize this was all a mistake.

Unlike the bathtub at home, this large steel tub had a metal bar across it with an attached tray. I had no earthly idea what to do with that bar and that tray. But I must say: the hot water felt better than anything had in a long time. Now that Nurse Robin knew for certain that there were no drugs or razors or knives, she smiled even more. Janet left the room only to return with a black tray. It looked like dinner. But why would she bring her dinner to the bathtubs? Also, why was I in this place and in this bathtub?

"It's for you."

"It's my dinner?"

"Your records show haven't been eating. You have been losing weight. You've been…nervous. The tub will relax you. You can start now. Start building yourself up, here in your new home."

In what home did they search you, tell you they'll shine lights in your eyes at all hours, serve you a meal in a steel bathtub.

Now, Dr. Regan. I imagined *he* was at home. He was enjoying his family. Regan. Irish? If so, maybe Catholic? He might be laying out his suit for church tomorrow. My own daddy would be whizzing off to Connecticut to some glittery rich person's party. He would be written up in the *Post*. In the social column. Or he was meeting one of those ladies he said hello to in the fancy restaurants. My father would be thinking of anything but me.

Meat in pale silky sauce. Potatoes and peas, bread and rice and apple juice *and* a small carton of milk. I ate as much as I could. Before the water could cool, I begged for the tray to be taken away. I lay back in the water and tried to put all the mad pieces together. What do I mean by mad? Everyone here must think I'm mad. It's the only reason they'd lock me up.

At least I didn't have to take a taxi anywhere. A taxi to some appointment or other. A cab that would rush and streak ahead while my heart pounded, while my nerves frayed and frayed while I really wanted to race back to the safety of home.

But maybe, just maybe, this was a safe place. At least until Monday. Dr. Regan would tell them there had been a huge mistake.

Janet looked up from checking her nail polish. She smiled at me. Like she had a secret. I understood that I would never know what that secret was.

Did I care? I was, right then, at risk of drowning while having dinner. No one drowns at dinner.

Then again. This might have been the place where all the other people—the other ones I hadn't seen yet—where all those mad people were. The only problem was that I was just wildly anxious when I had to leave my apartment. An inescapable fear, an attach of it, fear that might lead to sudden death, overcame me when I walked one block, two blocks, certainly three. I wasn't home then. I wasn't home now. I was sure, when I wasn't at home, that I would die.

Anything mad about that?

Hamptons Dinner Party

It was a brilliant day. The Hamptons at its best. Outside my lovely room all I could see was the reflection of the sun on the ocean and all I could hear was the sound of crashing waves. Another day in paradise and I was being paid to be there.

Later that morning I had the displeasure of seeing our too often houseguest, Shirley MacLaine. After five visits she still didn't know my name or why I was there. Just outside my window she pulled up her beach chair. For a second I thought she imagined that Andrew, my boss, was hard of hearing. But soon I understood that hearing had nothing to do with her constant need to whisper in his ear. It felt exactly like in the early grades of my all-girl school if a boy, for some reason, were to appear.

I decided I would ignore her presence as she ignored mine. I answered the morning mail, checked with the kitchen staff about that night's dinner party. Every Saturday summer evening these dinners were carefully thought out. Who we would entertain. What we would discuss. There were goals we hoped to accomplish. The evenings were far from just social. We were raising funds for Andrew's re-election. We were discussing bills on the books! These Saturday dinners were parties, sure, but they were also the only part of the weekend that was business. Not that pleasure didn't often accompany the evening.

One goal for that one evening: seat Shirley far away from Andrew. I'd had enough of the whisper campaign.

Another goal: an amazing meal. I had spoken to our wonderful cook and was assured that the menu we discussed was definite. The special wine had arrived. The dessert would be flaming.

Finally, arrangements were made and all was well in the world. I settled into the beach chair I had pulled into the shade and had opened the new book I'd been saving for a special time.

But I couldn't read. Not right away. I was too taken by the sense of how *lucky* I was to have landed such a great job with no credentials and no real experience. I had only, ever, needed *desire* and I could make things happen. I was a woman who could talk my way into anything. Yet never, never was I too sure of myself, never too confident: the ax was always about to fall.

Suddenly. Andrew standing over me, furious.

The two married couples we'd invited to engage and entertain our prospective donors had two different very valid reasons to cancel. They were bowing out. Kaput. According to Andrew this cancellation was entirely my fault. He glared and turned on his heel. I tossed down my book, ran into the house and began dialing. It was hopeless. Who of any importance at all would answer the phone on a Saturday afternoon and say yes, they were available for a dinner that same evening?

I dialed and I dialed. Andrew had spoken those dreaded words: YOUR JOB IS ON THE LINE.

Gone would be summers in all this luxury. Gone would be the chauffer-driven evenings and third row center tickets. Goodbye to all the many perks.

The pantry with the little shelf for the telephone was cool but I needed to wipe away the perspiration on my forehead and just then, just that suddenly, I realized this was exactly why I'd been hired. I was someone who came up with off the wall solutions, solutions that worked, solutions no one else would ever devise.

The next person I dialed? Dr. Arthur Korf. Not a *doctor* doctor. A dentist. He lived in Westhampton, thirty miles from us but *hours* away in Saturday evening, dinner-party traffic.

"Arthur," I said into the phone. "Something horrendous has happened."

"What, what." He was thinking medical emergency. "You're hurt?"

"No, NO," I gasped. "Worse. I need two couples for Andrew Stein's dinner in Easthampton. Tonight! You're the social commander of Westhampton. I just know you're going to help me out."

"What?" he practically yelled. "This late hour and you need someone who would join the horrendous traffic to Easthampton to show up for a dinner party?"

I took a deep breath. The idea was rising, the idea of offering her up—of offering her, the whisperer—as a kind of treat. "Tell them they'll meet two prominent New York couples. *And say that Shirley MacLaine is here.*"

"Give me half an hour."

I sat staring at the phone, perspiring profusely. Please, please let him call back with good news. I would so hate to be fired. Would they let me stay for the rest of the summer?

My watch seemed stuck. After an hour and a half, which seemed like five, the phone rang. "YES," I said.

"You owe me. Big time."

I really hoped that Dr. Korf, DDS, did not mean a sex debt.

"I found you a couple. He's also a dentist."

I swallowed hard. I could maybe introduce him as Dr. So-and-so? Andrew would understand.

"A dentist who's one hell of a dapper dresser. Big golfer. Lovely wife, a biology teacher."

I had no choice, but I had my doubts. There was simply no way I could tell Andrew that we still had no one, that we would have four empty places. With the dentist and his teacher-wife, we would have only two. Couldn't all the guests could talk about medicine? And, well—biology? Maybe there would be conversation about reproduction.

"Thank you. *Thank you.* Tell them seven on the dot." I needed them to arrive well before the other guests so I could figure the best way to fit them into the evening. Two lists: one of subjects to bring up, another of those to never. No religion, clearly, but yes to politics. Which could be difficult. There could be no *chance* of a rave about the other candidate for mayor. Andrew wanted the position so badly.

He reappeared in the doorway looking anxious. "Did you solve the problem?" He clearly expected that I had not.

"I surely did. A lovely doctor and his professor wife will be here at seven."

"G." Only Andrew called me that. He relaxed, brightened. "I got to hand it to you. You're not just a pretty face."

I didn't know if I loved that remark, but I had solved the problem.

I took a very long bath. I really was good at this. At solving problems. I dressed slowly. I checked on the kitchen and felt I could relax.

By quarter to seven I was sitting in the living room so I wouldn't miss the bell. At ten till, the doorbell rang. I jumped to open it.

I steadied myself. On sight of them, I thought I might faint. Here he was: a Dr. Goodly and his nervous wife, Belinda. He wore plaid golfing pants with a contrasting, totally clashing print short-sleeve shirt. Mrs. Dr. Goodly—on a Hamptons Saturday night at the height of summer—was entirely in black. It was as if she'd just stopped off at a funeral. Her heavy face was topped with a small black hat she'd decorated with a sprig of purple flowers that matched her eyeglass frames.

I wondered if I should run past these two and away, into the night.

"How was the traffic?" Without waiting for an answer, I said, "Please, do come in."

Settling himself onto the couch, Dr. G asked if he might have a drink. I couldn't chance taking them into the bar area where Andrew and late-afternoon colleagues might still be. I ran to the kitchen. I asked them to please bring out two glasses of tonic water with lime. I returned to the living room, making some sort of excuse as to why they weren't being offered a choice of beverage. These were, decidedly, not the type of people Andrew was expecting. I tried to make some conversation but my thoughts whirled.

Not that I had long to think. The door swung open and Andrew came in. My mouth had gone dry. I cleared my throat, heart beating rapidly. "Andrew. This is Dr. Goody and his professor wife Belinda."

His face went red. I knew what that meant. Without a single word he said, "I need to see you in the other room."

In the barroom he shut the door. "You have five minutes to get rid of those clowns. We'll talk when this is over. We'll be eight instead of twelve for dinner. This has taught me something about you."

Back in the living room, I said, "I don't know how to tell you this but something horrendous and personal has happened. I'll have to ask you to leave."

Dr. Golfer went white. "WHAT! You have us drive through Saturday night traffic, offer us tonic water and no hors d'oeuvres, then ask us to leave before dinner? We only came because Dr. Korf said it was a social emergency."

I thought quickly. I did have some Snickers bars in my bedroom. But that was not appropriate. A few See's lollypops? I was losing my mind.

"I am so, so sorry. Perhaps back in the city I could have you both as my guests to the South Seaport for a lovely lunch? Maybe I could arrange for passes to a musical. I could invite you to be my director friend's guest for *The Tonight Show?*"

"Young woman, you should be fired for this."

He had no idea how close I was to that.

"I'll—I'll—I'll report you!"

To The National Dental Society? "I am sorry. Please believe me when I say this is not really all my fault. I hope you'll find some way to forgive me. I'll make it up to you." I opened the front door. "Good luck with the traffic back."

Mrs. Dr. Golfer adjusted the hat that had begun to slide off one side. As she walked past she muttered that she'd never met anyone so rude and thoughtless.

I had to agree.

Andrew avoided me the entire evening, but some sort of luck was on my side. I will admit this: Shirley charmed the guests of honor like you would not believe. When they were leaving they complimented me for keeping the party so small. They had really gotten to know each other. It was the perfect evening. They had learned so much about our exciting election plans for the coming year. They said, "We feel we've cemented a lovely new friendship."

Standing in the pantry alone for a minute, I took a deep breath and willed myself to forget all that had happened.

Andrew's goodnight words: WELL DONE, G!

MARRIAGE TO A PRODUCER

Katherine was the best governess and housekeeper Paul and I ever had. She was from Panama with gorgeous dark hair and the longest natural eyelashes I had ever seen. She was so lovely. And came to work looking more chic than I did. Paul and I both shared her sense of humor. She knew all that was going on in our lives.

I was with producer Paul Heller—husband number four—and I was enjoying the life of a film producer's wife. But this isn't entirely true.

We had married on Fire Island. On the front page of the *Fire Island Post* we read "The Bride wore Sandals." It was a charming article. It was a good day. We had a great life in our brownstone in the Village and summers in Fire Island and while Paul's future was unsure then, we always dreamed that if everything fell through, we could and *would* love a year-round island life. Living off the coast of New York, he would be the year-round carpenter. He was as brilliant with his hands as he was producing films. I would find something I loved to do. I always did manage to find something that excited me.

When Katherine had been working for us for three years, when Jami was just about to turn five, new projects came up for Paul. Jami was my daughter. Not Paul's. Though he was wonderful with her. Much to Paul's delight and my dismay, the films might mean a move to Los Angeles. If he took the jobs, I would have to begin thinking of husband number five, as I would hate the West and any chance of leaving New York was appalling.

But this is a story about Katherine.

Always, she dressed Jami like an angel. She gave her these hair-dos, really very pretty, woven with real flowers she'd bring from the flower shop. Sometimes she'd sew Jami a new dress that was beyond chic. Her own style was so elegant, and life with her around was such joy. Jami was her main job, but she helped us enormously with phone calls, messages, organizing. Everything that made the New York house feel like a home. All that made our lives feel like the dreams they were.

That month of June, when Jami was five, Paul had put the Los Angeles opportunities aside for an amazing script he developed. It was a film that would take place on Ischia, an island some hours from Rome. Things would be pretty frantic on Ischia, especially with a tight shooting schedule. We were to first spend several days in Rome where some initial scenes would be shot.

There, in Rome, the always great Katherine and my polite daughter become the pets of the hotel. They were everyone's favorites. Lovely as the hotel was, we were surprised when a great deal of noise and commotion happened each afternoon. Four young men with long hair in a somewhat odd style descended from upper suites to wade through the crowds that had been gathering all day to see them. I couldn't understand all the screaming, all the applause. They were small young men, slight, boyish. The concierge claimed they were singers, quite known in Europe. But why all the fuss for four young men from Liverpool?

We hardly managed getting back and forth to the pool, but that didn't bother us. Katherine who, as always, had everything planned to keep Jami amused and happy if we were working on set. She kept our lives in order as well.

There were, as with all films, many problems to be solved. Paul was wonderful enough to weather the usual temperaments, the upsets with the couturier, unexpected thunderstorms, everything was handled with calm. Any annoyance he might have had was saved for his wife, but I rarely let that get to me as it didn't happen often. It was actually whenever our lives became secure and quite good that my mind would wander to who might end up being the next husband. Longevity was not my strong suit.

Being a producer's wife was a new challenge, a life I had never imagined at Finch Junior College. I was the kind of New York girl who thought going to Fire Island was leaving for a new country. I had never felt the desire to travel or see the world. Why would I? New York was everything. Nice Jewish girls from the Westside with their private schools only needed to think about secure marriages and bringing up little girls who would be just like them.

I had never been out of the United States, and though I kept expecting everyone to speak English I coped when I had a translator. Because my father was a famous clothing designer, and because I had been a model, I knew the garment district. I knew couture and how it was created. I took to it naturally when Paul asked me to step in as a stylist. Organizing wardrobe was second nature to me and I loved the work. I dressed Diane Cilento, Alan Bates and the rest of the cast. We were so busy fitting trousers, skirts, hats and all the costume jewelry that had to be coordinated to each outfit. I spent a part of each day with the wardrobe designer. It was like stepping into the pages of *Vogue*. Here I was, in Rome, Italy, experiencing all this wonder. Meanwhile, fabulous Katherine kept Jami happy.

"Paul, I think we should leave Katherine and Jami in the hotel here while we set things up in Ischia. We can arrange for them to take the boat and meet us in a few days."

"Good idea," said Paul who wasn't listening. Children, let alone mine from another marriage, were never the first thing on his mind in the middle of a production.

So, Paul and I would go. A few days later a car would bring Katherine and Jami to the boat, the boat would bring them to the island, another car would bring them to our hotel. We all instructed Katherine about the car from the hotel to the boat, about the boat, about taking a taxi to the Villa Paradiso on Ischia, which we wrote down of course. She had all details tucked in her handbag.

The night before the cast and crew left for Ischia, there was such a good feeling among the actors that I saw the lovely and exciting side of film production. We were a family. Or far better: a group of the closest friends. I loved group living. I always had. That's just what this was—or was it? What would happen when the film was over and everyone went back to their own lives? But I was so happy. I felt loved and all was glorious. Why wonder what came next?

I had so *much* to think about. I had chosen the wardrobe. There could be no costume changes now that we were leaving Rome. Would the female co-star feel slighted by the broad-striped silk I had chosen for the third scene? Would I run out of Valium? Were there doctors on small Italian islands who might refill American prescriptions if the American wife of an important movie producer were to find herself entirely undone? There was, I reminded myself as I packed in our Roman hotel, no reason in the world that would be a possibility. I was happy.

When we boarded the boat the next morning, I ran to hug my daughter who began to cry when I said, "Mommy is going away for a couple of days or so, but you'll be coming to meet me."

I told her Katherine had a big surprise for her. We found someone who would take them to the zoo!

"Mommy." She looked serious, like a small adult. But also, like a very young child. "Are you sure that all the same animals will be at this zoo? Are you sure I'll get to see the same kinds of animals we see in Central Park?" When I said, "Yes," she jumped up and down with happiness. We had a few tight hugs and I was on my way.

Ischia was beautiful. The set was gorgeous. Each outfit I had chosen fit well and the stars and cast seemed happy. There on the small Italian island, my role complete, I allowed myself to "relax," an activity I rarely indulged.

Before I knew it, Tuesday had arrived. Katherine and Jami would be coming in on the last boat. It was to arrive at five. The taxi ride up narrow streets to the hotel took ten minutes. Just before five I stood waiting in the front entrance hall, right by the front door. I couldn't help but keep glancing at my watch. It was five, then five-thirty. Then it was almost six.

I needed to find Paul. Surely he had heard something that would explain what had to be a simple delay.

"Paul! Paul!" I shouted as I pushed through the door to our room. "Katherine and Jami. They've been kidnapped." Suddenly in my mind this was the only truth. "It's all your fault bringing me to this crazy place for a movie. My child is gone!"

Paul was not unused to my anxiety. He tried to calm me. He was sure all would be clear in a moment. He telephoned the boat basin and was assured that the boat had, in fact, already arrived.

"Do something!" I was sobbing. "Call the police. They have to know something."

He did just that. They knew nothing. They would call with any news.

We waited in silence for the phone to ring.

He called the police again. No word. From anyone.

I took more Valium. I couldn't breathe.

The phone rang.

Paul pressed it to his ear, listened. "Who did you say? Peter? Peter Sellers?"

I grabbed the telephone.

"This is Paul's wife. Who is this really?"

A calm, caring voice said, "This is still Peter Sellers. I have a lovely little girl here named Jami. She's with her very caring nanny, Katherine. They just had some ice cream and a few cookies and they gave me your name. I said I'd help find you. They said you were on the island. As am I. Seems we're both making films here. You have a lovely little girl. I'm about to put her and Katherine in a car to your hotel."

I was crying so hard I handed Paul the phone without even thanking Peter Sellers so much for his caring.

He and Paul spoke about productions, about the coincidence of working in Ischia at the same time. Paul laughed and told Peter some things about our film, then sat nodding and listening. He hung up and said he would go downstairs to wait for the car.

Time had never gone so slowly.

Finally, Katherine and Jami were through the hotel door. Jami ran into my arms, happy and very ready to tell me all about her adventures. Katherine stood silently, entirely upset, so very sad. Making no noise, she cried and cried.

"Katherine," I held Jami tight in my lap. "Whatever is wrong?"

Her tears did not stop.

"Please. What's wrong?"

"I never told you something. All this time." She looked to Paul. "I didn't tell either of you. I never learned to read. I can't read and when you left me the instructions to get here, I couldn't read a word. I can't hide this from you anymore. I didn't want you to know. Now you know. I love you all, but I am prepared to leave and to say my goodbyes." She could not stop crying. "I know you'll fire me."

"Fire you? Katherine, we love you dearly. We could never never manage without you! You're part of our crazy family. We want you with us forever, and when we get back to New York a teacher will come to the house and teach you to read and write."

"Katherine." It was Paul's turn. He really could be so kind. "Katherine. You know we love you. I'll take you both to your new room and you'll do Jami's favorite thing—order room service. And guess what? There's a pool here too. Tomorrow? A swimming day."

I was so grateful to see my precious Jami and wonderful Katherine.

And you know, Paul wasn't bad either. Even Peter Sellers liked him. He might have been someone to keep after all.

THE VIOLA WOLFE DANCING SCHOOL

Today my favorite shoes are the ones I'm wearing right now. They have supportive arches and are so comfortable. They might not be attractive, but they're easy to take on and off, especially when travelling, and perfect for my morning walks.

But how do they compare with the patent leather flats with the side buttons I wore when I was ten and was forced to attend Viola Wolfe dancing school for young girls who might one day have a place in society?

My hair was always frizzy on those Friday nights and I always had to hide a band-aid stuck to me somewhere after playing on the rocks in Central Park. My skirt always seemed too long or too short.

Always, I hoped it would be a good night.

The girls sat in a long line of chairs. When the music began, we waited for the boys to come ask us to dance. It was frightening. What if nobody picked me? If they did, what would I talk about? This was not a splendid time. I never had any brothers or boy cousins, so I knew nothing about what to say to a boy my age. Also, I went to an all-girls school.

Well, that Friday night Neal Anderson, the cutie of the class, was approaching. He was really heading my way. He was going to ask me to dance. My hands got sweaty and I could feel myself blushing. He was really very cute—though quite short. I was taller than all the girls. This would be an advantage in my later years, or so my ballet teacher had said, but at that moment, my cheeks felt purple. He did as he had been instructed to do: asked me to dance.

So I began to stand up. When I rose and rose to finally loom three feet taller than he was, Neal said, quite loudly, "No thank you!" and walked away.

My hands turned to ice. There was not one uncounted-for boys left in this round. I had no partner and would have to sit alone on the chairs. Everyone would see me.

I vowed then that if I ever learned to dance and was ever invited to any parties, I wouldn't be happy about it at all. Next Friday night I planned to eat two boxes of candy and be too sick to attend.

My chances with any boys seemed extinct. And that was just fine with me.

Jazz at Noon

It was already Thursday and we'd had no confirmation of any special guests for our "Jazz at Noon" tomorrow.

As always, we had our bass, piano, and drums covered by musicians we hired—any of whom would step away if a famous jazz-playing "guest" happened in. Some Fridays we invited names, other days we counted on fate. Woody Allen, Lionel Hampton, Django Reinhardt, and George Shearing had all played with us, just to name a few. No money was paid to any guest musicians. They would just show up. For them it was just a great gig. We didn't exactly advertise that the rest of the band was made up of neighborhood businessmen, doctors, dentists, and ad agency players who loved jazz enough to play for free. Decidedly, their first love was jazz even if supporting families or other responsibilities had led them down different paths. Of course my co-founder Les was there with his competence, his penny whistle and his clarinet. You never knew who you might hear on Friday jam sessions. Our chef was one of the best and our luncheon menu very special.

As luck would have it, the day we didn't have a name was a day that looked packed. My girlfriend Rhoda arrived early, revving up her pursuit to capture the attention of my partner Les. Les was married to a woman who was sure that *I* was the one wanting to sleep with him. Always, she was reminding me she was, "Les's wife, you know."

It was well after one o'clock and the sounds of dining and conversation were everywhere. Les looked pale. I had just resolved the anger of four of our best customers who'd arrived late for their usual table, a table that was filled.

Why on earth, I asked myself, did I drink that cup of tea in Fire Island with Les and allow him to talk me into partnering in this club? I could be *home* Friday afternoons. I could be preparing for the weekend with no stress and no surprises. With no *lack* of surprises.

I was passing the front door on my way toward Les when I saw an elderly man with close-cropped gray hair. He looked like he could be in his eighties. He was asking something of a pleasant looking woman who was waiting in the doorway for her cab. He was very soft-spoken, but I heard his accent—French—from where I stood.

Nearing them, I smiled at the woman and asked the gentleman, "Can I help you?"

"Well yes. Yes. I read about your club in the *Post*. I thought I might sit in today."

"That might just work out well. That might work very nicely. Might I have your name?"

"I am… Stéphane Grappelli."

Of course. I *knew* I knew that voice. Suddenly it was all too much.

The man standing before me—was none other than *the* pre-eminent European-born jazz violinist. Stéphane Grapelli had played the Newport Jazz Festival when I was a publicist. He was from Paris. Self-taught, for the most part, he had played with the renowned Django Reinhardt, the two of them inventing their very own brand of jaunty swinging jazz. Their quintet was "Du Hot Club," legendary in all of France. All of Europe. All the *world*.

The fact was, all famous American jazz players had played in Europe. Europe understood before America, even back in the 30s, that jazz was a supremely important music. All our musicians had gone to live where jazz was revered, few in the States having realized the value of this music. When war was coming, Stéphane settled in London playing with none other than the great piano-genius George Shearing. And now the man stood before me.

"Mr. Grappelli. Stéphane. I am so honored to welcome you to our club."

He was very shy. Very *sweet*. "I would love to play. It would be my great pleasure. But maybe just don't announce me."

"But Stéphane." Already it felt like we were the closest of friends. At least, that I was the most reverent of fans. "Everyone will be on their feet applauding the minute you take the stage!"

He shook his head, slowly. "That's all right. Just please. Don't announce me."

You should know, at this point, I had a double reason for wanting him announced. Some half hour earlier I had seated a *Times* reporter at the perfect, most intimate, most lovely table for one. The reporter was looking entirely bored, totally impatient, reading notes he'd taken—surely from another gig. He'd hardly looked up from his little pad.

And now Stéphane, *the* Stéphane Grappelli, *my Stéphane*, had specifically requested that I not announce him.

I wondered if I might take the initiative to not announce the great man, but maybe to simply go over and tell the bored reporter of Signore Grappelli's arrival?

Better not. Because there was yet another piece to this puzzle. Not just Stéphane, but the reporter had made it clear when *he* arrived that he would like to be a simple audience member, an anonymous being, not anything like official press. One had to wonder, by the look on his face, if the man even liked jazz.

At least we were doing good business, even if *The Times* wasn't going to have the name to prove all the fun of this "Noon" session. Maybe the chef could put an upper in the man's chicken pot pie?

The reporter, after all, wasn't that different from many others that preferred to stay remote. And now—too bad—there was also the couple talking loudly at the bar. This couple, the eternal couple, sat at our bar thinking nothing at all about jazz. They must have imagined they'd come across a convenient place to stop in for a drink, completely oblivious of the music.

Stéphane, though, now *he* was unusual.

I took my hand from his arm, promised I'd be right back, and rushed across the room—smiling at some people, artfully dodging others—to approach Les. "You'll never imagine. Guess who's here to sit in. He just arrived just now. *Stéphane Grappelli*."

For the briefest of flashes Les looked gravely disappointed.

Then I understood. This was not disappointment. This was disbelief.

His thrill was contagious. We were both equally struck. The mere thought.

And soon Stéphane—a little stooped, a little shuffly, eighty if he was a day—was climbing up the couple of steps to the stage. There was a hush. When he began tuning the violin he carried in a battered black case, even the reporter took notice.

What a moment.

I so wish—now, today—that we had recorded, even just for us, some of those sessions.

Les had come down with a slight cold the night before but he had always assured me that he could play even with whooping cough. He got on that penny whistle and was brilliant as always. There was a loud drum roll, the piano with its quick intro on one of Grappelli's most famous numbers from the Hot Club, and we were off.

It was some of the most thrilling sounds that room of jazz lovers ever had the pleasure of hearing. Stéphane himself might have been missing Yehudi Menuhin or André Previn, masters with whom he had just recorded. But he looked happy enough, having no idea that the great talents playing with him now were a vice president from Goldman Sachs on vibes, a Levi's ad rep on drums, the head of NYPD on sax, the piano manned by a Wall Street mogul, and my sinus doctor on trombone.

I was so thrilled. I was so *moved*, that I managed to spill the cola I was holding, missing the shoulder of one of our regulars who would have not appreciated that shower in any way at all. I managed to quiet the couple at the bar by promising dessert and a full round of drinks when the session was over if they might please hold their conversation.

"Who is that guy anyway?" the loud talker asked.

"Oh"—I waved a casual hand, leaned close—"just a jazz great from Paris."

His girlfriend swiveled toward Stéphane, the banker, Dr. Ear, Nose, and Throat—her mouth a little open. She turned back. "Paris, *France?*"

But I was already making my way to the back where I could watch and listen in peace.

It was a spell he held over us all. His eyes closed, he wore a slight smile, like maybe he was dreaming, or very far away.

I myself forgot to wonder if we were making or losing money. Did it matter if there were fewer chicken pot pies than we needed? Did I care if Les's wife would accuse me, yet again, of sleeping with her husband? Just staying awake with that man could be annoying sometimes.

I thought of Grappelli and Reinhardt, then, in an old gray country. I imagined how they must have been loved and how they had broken up when it looked like Hitler was going to invade France.

The sets went on and on, until the early evening. No one wanted the master to quit. Never had any of our musicians sounded so good. I overheard one young man confessed to another, "I'll probably be fired for not getting back to the office—but for this moment, do I care?"

The applause seemed like it would never stop either. But eventually the day was ending. When the old master, in his gray trousers and gray sweater finally stepped to the front of the stage and took a deep, European-style bow, my eyes filled. I had heard a jazz on this Friday. I had presented a musical genius to a room full of grateful listeners who had stayed well past when they had planned to leave.

And honestly. Who knew what the next week might bring?

This was New York. This was my jazz club. This was my biggest distraction from the world of thinking about the next lover, the next possible husband—if there were to be one.

Sometimes only jazz can do that.

BREAKFAST IN THE NEW YORK DINER

My friend Allie called as I was leaving the house last Tuesday. She must talk to me. "Extremely personal," she said.

"Of course. I'll be at the usual." Allie understood this was the diner. The Hudson. At Hudson and Barrow.

Allie is much younger than I. For some wonderful reason, at 89, I have a group of younger friends who seem to love being with me. They enjoy my advice on many topics but mainly on how to deal with the men in their lives. They view me as having a PhD in love relationships. Maybe because I've had so many.

*

My husband and I had gotten up early that Tuesday morning. I was supposed to go with him to the gym. Though my guy is in his later years, he thinks he's a jock. I do love how sporty he looks in his $400 sneakers but my nerves decided they'd do better with pancakes than entering a gymnasium where I would run to nowhere or row on no water. Who needs all that loud music or the trainer screaming, "Three more rounds! Abs! Now thighs!" My abs were nonexistent and as for thighs, well, no thank you.

The gym routine was just to keep our marriage going. Togetherness. But sometimes the gym just made me think of calling my old boyfriend. He had just gotten divorced and while he was fat and could never be called "in good shape," he understood that even weekday mornings were for the *Times*, croissants with butter and jam

51

and the important decision of which film for later in the evening. I have always been happier with an intellect, with someone who loved the arts. Why did I ever leave that man for an "athlete"?

I arrived before Allie. There is nothing like overhearing bits of conversations at the Hudson. I found myself becoming part of the many stories taking place over breakfast.

At the table not two feet to my right, an elderly man sat across from another elderly man. I had seen them before. Sitting sipping tea.

The heavier one held an unlit cigar. "How terrible for her. I guess what the doctors hoped never did happen."

"Well. You know she still hears voices."

"How you must suffer."

"At least she doesn't answer them." And in the next breath he ordered poached eggs on rye, bacon well done, double coffee—all as his companion was quite silent. As I guess I was too.

A young and lovely looking mother, little girl always a bit out of control, moved past. Her good morning nod seeming apologetic in advance of what might be the morning's crisis.

Which was when Allie arrived.

*

She adjusted her bra strap, flung her bag onto the wooden chair across from me. She sat, looking a mess, flushed, eyes teary. She seemed so sad, so *distraught* that I couldn't even ask, would you like anything to eat?

Her man had not called her back.

"Just because you haven't heard from him in five days after that wild night"—Allie had shown up with the whip and the latex cat suit that she and her man thought they would enjoy—"that doesn't mean it's all over."

"How does it not?"

"Let me tell you: this coffee is awful. I really ought to send it back."

"You're worried about the coffee?" Her voice was full of sadness, but at 89 I had learned it was good to worry about coffee. It was important: worrying about coffee puts things in perspective. I knew for certain that this man was not for Allie. I felt she knew it. Deep down.

"Please, though," she was saying. "You're so good on relationships."

"Yes. I am. But what you're telling me doesn't give me any clue what went wrong. What's he looking for. Maybe he's allergic to latex? I've heard some patients die from the doctor's rubber gloves during surgery."

Her tears welled.

"You have to know I'm only teasing. Let me ask you, has he always needed more than just exciting, loving sex? What have his other relationships been like? Was he ever married? Because I know you. Showing up with a whip and a cat suit to please someone does not sound like the love you're looking for. You want companionship. Someone to share your interests. You need a theatre lover!"

"So, I should know more about him. I should call him? To find out more about who he is."

It wasn't exactly what I'd meant. I said, "That would be good. Also—find out if he's allergic."

She laughed a little and eventually we got to speaking about my upcoming art exhibit and her acting classes. We talked about the role she'd just landed at the SoHo Playhouse. I told her she'd be absolutely amazing and maybe by then she'd have three new suitors to replace Mr. Whips and Chains. "With your talent and looks"—I really meant it—"the world can be yours."

*

It was getting late.

Allie had to run.

I had an appointment later that morning on Wall Street. My broker said it was too late for gold but every last person in my office—when they weren't not talking about production schedules and raising capital for the new building—they were discussing what they'd made on gold.

I sat waiting for the check, alone. I thought about how my broker was a good broker. He wore a yarmulke, was Orthodox. I wondered if there was anything in Torah studies that related to never buying gold. But then, look at all the Jews on 47th selling gold jewelry with and without diamonds. He told me the market couldn't go any higher. He said he was being conservative to protect me. I had made almost nothing in six months.

Sitting, waiting, I thought about how much I would've preferred French toast or pancakes. I hadn't order either. Not after all those months of Fit-for-Life. I was losing money, longing for fattening food. It looked like rain and I had no umbrella. I would have to take the subway downtown. I would have loved nothing more than a limousine.

Also, should I wonder why my husband picked that divine blonde as his personal trainer? I mean, just how personal were we talking? I understood very well, though, that it wasn't smart for me to be wasting energy on that. I knew he loved me.

*

I felt the sense—waiting for the check, thinking of real Vermont maple syrup—that we were all in this together.

This was the morning of another Tuesday in the best city in the world, a city with a sense of life force like no other place on the planet.

The diner had grown very crowded, very noisy. I felt ever so much a part of all that surrounded me. This was my city; this was my life.

You've Won

She walked into the apartment that night and the TV was on, endless news blaring but not being watched. He sat on the couch in a corner of the most beautiful loft in the entire Village. All around him were papers.

He looked up. "Hey Gorgeous. Good day? I missed you. How was rehearsal? Looks like things went well. Let's see those legs. Skirt's too long."

After pulling the skirt up to mid-thigh, knowing that he loved her for more than just her legs, then letting it drop, she sat next to him, papers be damned.

He pulled her close. Then let her go. He smiled at her like maybe she was the best thing he had seen even at the end of a good long day. How exciting he was. Older, yes, but eyes so alive. Energy and power glowed around him like a halo.

In the past, of course, through the decades, he'd been a womanizer. But now this dynamic powerful man wanted only her.

He had asked her to choose the most amazing of all the Village lofts, even when, for him, there was no life below 57th Street. But the loft was what she wanted, so that was what he asked her to choose. She had fallen in love: first with him, of course, but then with the raised-platform meditation room created by the former guru tenant, and with its incredible view of the Hudson and magnificent parquet floors. Because of her figure and long blond hair, it would seem she made many things he laughed at acceptable to him. Such as the former guru's tenants enclosed prayer room, herbal medicine, acupuncture, natural healing. He had always been, after all, a man of the streets. He'd made his millions without the help of the new age beliefs, and though he made attempts to stifle any reference she might make to vegetarian restaurants, health food stores or any form of self-searching, he was the man of her dreams. And now, at long last—to the utter despair of quite a few New York ladies—he was all hers!

Besides, if she ever felt weak or vulnerable, or heaven forbid *not well*, she had her apartment to escape to. It was nearby. There, she would regroup, work on getting her insecurity in control. He hated any need for emotional reassurance. She would escape. She would then return only as Miss Wonderful-All-Accepting-NeverFragile-Woman-of-Sophistication-and-Excitement. Not the needy, needing a roof over her head woman she really was.

But now, here on the couch, he had just said something to her in such a very serious tone.

She looked into his great blue-grey eyes, and thought, tonight? He might propose now? Her grey roots were showing, after she missed the salon appointment because she was looking for his favorite croissants and the newest *Financial Times* to bring him tonight. After a very busy day, gray was not at all sexy, and sexy was what he seemed to need from her at all times. She held her breath. Timing wasn't everything. Was this the moment?

"I have cancer," he said. "I need a kidney removed. It'll be at Sloan Kettering next week."

There was no way to fight back the tears of possible loss of this hero, this only man in her world who she might ever love this passionately. She gasped. "Darling. Darling. I am here for you. In body and soul. Twenty-four hours a day. I will never let anything happen to you. I will be at your side, at the hospital every minute. When you get home, too. I'll cancel my projects and try to delay the opening. I'll help you with your work." She would promise everything in the universe, short of being the patient instead of him. "I will help while you're getting strong—I mean *stronger*. Back in, as you call it, Michael-Fighting-Shape!"

"Hey." He patted her gently on her back, like they were two acquaintances at a foundation board meeting. "Hey. Hey. That's not going to work at all."

"What? Darling. You know how devoted I am to you, to us, to our future, I…"

"Yes. Yes I do know. But this is going to be different"

"What does that mean?"

"There's a chance, at my age, I don't come through this."

"Oh no. No." She wanted to shout, but spoke softly, knowing that he hated, as he called it, a woman out of control of her emotions. "You're so strong," she told him, "You jog three times a week, you never eat cholesterol. You live for your work. You love this new loft and your…grandchildren."

"As I was saying, before you interrupted"—he looked, maybe, a bit angry—"at my age there are no guarantees." They were back in the board room. He was now talking with his business voice. "I plan to use this time in the hospital, and perhaps some time after, at home, while recuperating, to see all the women I've loved in my life. Including ex-wives. Listen. You've never been possessive. It's one of the things I love so much about you. I know you'll understand."

The seventh floor was actually quite high. If there were a guarantee, now, of death—sudden, immediate—then the window over his shoulder might do. *His* death, not hers. Could she push him out? A tantrum? But that would never do. Georganne had made an *art form* of keeping herself together. Suddenly, though, she felt unattractive, useless, insecure. She was, all at once, back in competition with all the beautiful, powerful, good-looking women in this enormous city of cities. How would she be all right with this idea? The idea that their wonderful romance might be removed with that kidney?

"Come now." Michael had seen her shrink like Alice into a tiny creature right before his eyes. "You're a mature woman. No time for carrying on here. Matter of fact, where shall we go for dinner once I catch the end of the news? Now you be a good little girl, Daddy's little girl. Put on a shorter skirt, you know I love those beautiful legs. Find us a romantic place for dinner."

Daddy's little girl! He wouldn't *reach* Sloan Kettering. If not the window then a knife, poison, strangulation. The rotten lousy son-of-a-bitch dream wrecker.

But really…her heart was splintering into a thousand pieces. She would precede him to the hospital. They would check her in. They would say amongst themselves: How on earth could this healthy woman be expiring right here in the emergency room with no noticeable signs of any illness at? Is it emotional shock?

"Oh yes," she said. "I understand. Where would you like to go to dinner?"

He grabbed her and kissed her on her trembling lips then said "Feel like fish?"

She wished she *were* a fish, a goldfish, happy to swim aimlessly in her bowl.

*

How could she begin to describe the scene in the hospital. When she arrived he was in his bed waiting for the pre-ops. Standing over him was a tall, dynamic, spirited woman. She seemed totally in charge. It must be Gloria, one of his ex-wives.

He'd left this most recent wife after eighteen years. He'd said she was a powerful woman but even Georganne didn't expect that the she would almost demand they all salute. Even the insecure-looking young intern, who kept asking if it was all right to examine the patient, seemed nervous.

"You'll do no such thing!" the ex commanded. "I'm in charge here. Only Dr.

Samerset will look at him. Where's the private nurse I hired? I will not accept this type of inefficiency! I'm here to be sure he has the best care."

All Georganne could think while standing and staring was, boy, she must have been one dramatic lay. The very sight of her would make most men impotent.

But not Michael. He was a decorated soldier from the Second World War, a real war. Nothing was too challenging for her man.

The ex turned, "And who are you?" Not waiting for Georganne's answer, she turned back to the bed. "Don't worry, Michael. I'm here now. When you come out of this we'll take you back home and get you all spruced up."

Spruced up! As a total city dweller, she had only ever heard those words on the farm she once visited for the night in Hillsdale

New York, with her date, a New York celebrity dentist. Not a doctor-doctor, but a dentist-doctor. Also—home to whose house?

And to think Georganne had been told just days before by Michael's grown daughter that apparently, this ex was in fact, still, Michael's wife. The divorce papers he filed had either not been read, or were discarded as one more meaningless threat. Georganne was still trying to deal with that information.

Maybe it was that fact that made her run home through the December cold after leaving the hospital. She had not eaten since she was told of Michael's illness and his recovery plan. In her apartment she called girlfriends to ask for help. She sobbed on the telephone till she had no tears left and fell asleep feeling very alone, by herself in her own apartment.

The next morning was grey, dismal. She made her way uptown to the hospital. Michael's operation had been that morning. All had gone well though there was still the threat of something. Infection, recurrence, another small procedure might be necessary? As she approached Michael's room, a woman stopped her.

"Hello there. You're Georganne, aren't you?"

"Well, yes. I am. I'm not sure we've met before."

"I'm Gilda. Michael's first wife, mother of Janet and Elise? We met at the Christmas party?"

Of course they had? Gilda was *that* memorable. If this woman before her was the challenge, Georganne had won not only the set, but the entire match. The Connecticut country club upbringing she had made her sometimes talk in tennis terms, no matter what the situation!

"Of course. Of course. You're Gilda!"

Now here was a respite from the panic and shortness of breath, from the thought that she wasn't strong enough to handle all that might take place—from the female point of view, it would be a sure win. Poor Gilda! That vintage hat with the veil that got stuck to her mouth, requiring her to adjust it as she spoke. Her dress looked out of a Sears catalogue, despite what must have been enough alimony to purchase any outfit on Madison Avenue. She looked like maybe all the money was going to animal shelters, the Yeats Society, or help for abused women. Georganne had been told in the past that she was judgmental, that she jumped to conclusions. She wondered if that was true. Still, this Fashion Disaster seemed soft, kind and lovely, all traits Michael would never notice if the package didn't suit his current image of the "perfect" woman. For Michael a woman had to be great socially and always a "knock-out." But hey, he had two children with Gilda, while he was working his way through law school, living in the tenement flats and being called "Mikey," which he hated, by all his neighbors in Queens.

She took a deep breath and reminded herself that Michael had a tough beginning being brought up in a foster home. Maybe now, sick, he wanted to return to the comfort of this intellectual earth mother with Birkenstocks and huge breasts. But would Gilda ever possibly do as a partner for his political fundraisers? Of course not.

Now, here, Gilda was saying, "Georganne, I'd like to talk to you privately. Can we sit down in the waiting room? Before I see him?"

Georganne's lips were suddenly dry, in desperate need of balm. Honestly, what could be worse than the hospital waiting area: television blaring, horrendous lighting, the smell of stale coffee, kids trying to amuse themselves while saying, "Daddy, Daddy can we go now? How long? How *long* till Mommy's ready to leave?" What could this soft round ex-wife want to ask Georganne in such a place? She had no time for this. Her campaign hinged on showing Michael how smart and special she was. She needed to tell him the headline she caught on the *Wall Street Journal* on the way over through the wintery morning; he needed to know the Dow was down twenty points. She ought to demonstrate, soon, now, that even in her rush to be with him, she was a woman who stayed well informed about politics and finance.

But wait. Was she mad? If she told him, "The Dow! It dropped twenty!" Michael would have a heart attack. Although. Then she'd be free? Or would she?

She steadied herself, a hand against the wall, to make way for a patient with his walker, catheter trailing, who moved by on the arm of a very attractive young brunette. His daughter? Georganne wanted to see Michael but the need to concentrate on Gilda seemed more urgent.

Just entering through the waiting room door, Georganne was nearly crippled by a toy truck sent careening across the floor by a small boy. But Gilda didn't laugh at her. Gilda was so sympathetic, so kind that Georganne could imagine nothing but this woman saving Michael from many an emotional fall. Even back then, was he dreaming of the days when suburban life would be over, and he'd be a major force on the political scene? After realizing she was no threat, Georganne realized that liked this ex-wife.

But why did Gilda need to talk to her alone? There was Gilda with her comfortable shoes, while Georganne's feet were so confined in her high heels, they'd never recognize comfort again. Gilda had the look of a one who enjoyed being a martyr. But then, who was Georganne to talk? Running her business and sitting here with Mrs. Sears Catalogue in a crowded waiting room, with a sense of panic coming over her, while she didn't have the strength to call her office, and see if Bloomingdale's had called in that expected re-order, or if that Japanese fabric had arrived. After all, if she lost Michael, she wouldn't care about shipping clothing to any store at all. Why even to go to work? Why get up in the morning? She was not going to allow herself to think about a Michael-less future!

The mission was exhausting. She was trail blazing alone. Even missions that take you to war zones involve a team and a planned front-line attack. The only attack here was the possibility of there being a more appealing woman in Michael's room with an offer of twenty-four-hour wild sex, great legs and a huge prominent group of wealthy politicians to introduce him to: that would help the fund-raisers for senators he was backing, which would leave her without the man of her dreams. She had to deal with this crisis alone.

"Yes, Gilda. What is it?"

The woman's eyes filled with tears, but of course she was prepared with a tidy Kleenex Pack. "He might not pull through this operation, you know. If he doesn't, I need to make sure that I'm the one buried beside him." Georganne was overwhelmed with Gilda's kindness and loving request. Georganne had no desire whatsoever to be buried by the man. To go through the anxiety of not being his only love on this planet was enough.

"Gilda. Michael's very strong. He seems to be doing well. I'm sure he'll pull through with no problems."

"Oh please." She began to sob. "Please."

"He hasn't discussed these plans with me, but of course I'll be sure to bring this up as soon as possible. You can count on that."

"Oh you are a darling. My girls said you were. So understanding. Now, I've some homemade kreplach and soup. Here in this thermos."

Oh my God. The very sight of the Jewish food he'd abandoned after he left Queens for Sutton Place—that would be worse than mentioning the Dow! What politician business mogul sat in bed eating kreplach from a thermos? And how could she tell Gilda that Michael didn't want to talk with her while he was alive now, so why would he want to talk to her when he was dead? Georganne felt so not threatened by sweet Gilda that she asked her, "Can I get you a cup of tea? I'm going to the cafeteria." Insecurity was certainly a state that Georganne could relate to. "Maybe something for you to eat?"

Georganne herself would be having a salad with no dressing, a Diet Coke, and black coffee. While Michael would be upstairs convalescing, she would stare longingly at cakes and French toast and her favorite mac-and-cheese.

"Oh no dear," said Gilda. "You told me what I wanted to hear. Thank you. I think I'll go visit Michael now that I have that weight lifted from me."

Georganne thought maybe Gilda really should have a little weight lifted off of her but being thin could not be that important.

Gilda stood. "It's been so lovely speaking with you. We are all in this together." Was this a newly formed high school basketball team? And how many were yet to join the game?

*

They might all be in it together but Georganne was coming apart!

She entered the cafeteria quite ill at ease. The long talk with Gilda and this trip meant she was leaving her territory too unguarded for too long a time. Still, though, she took a seat with her tray and got out her copy of *Cosmopolitan*, the one she hadn't wanted Michael to see. She needed to study the lead article: "HOW TO HANDLE THE UNFAITHFUL MALE."

But Michael wasn't being unfaithful now, was he? How unfaithful could he be? The man would still have a catheter.

She spent more time on the article than she expected to. It was fascinating, learning how to beat the odds on infidelity from women who always triumphed. The coffee was weak, awful, but what she read was practical, gripping. Still, all at once she put the magazine down. Without her guarding Room 609, what with Michael not in full command of himself, he might have even liked the kreplach in its thermos. He might have regressed to Mickey from Queens Boulevard.

She rushed from the table like the fire alarm had gone off and bumped into an intern carrying a tray of fries. Food cascaded over the linoleum floor.

"I am so sorry," she said, stepping on a fry. "But I just got an emergency text from the sixth floor." She wasn't sure why she was lying. "I didn't even see you."

He looked exhausted, and not very understanding, but she imagined he'd just come from resuscitating someone. She felt suddenly, entirely humiliated. "Can I buy you another serving of French fries?"

"No. Thank you." He could not get away from her quickly enough.

*

In the elevator, in her haste, now sweating, she pushed the alarm button instead of six. One contact lens had come out during the night so her sight was limited. In her anxiety, she was also now shaking, which seemed to terrify the passengers crowding into the elevator with her. General visiting hours had begun. For some reason, the little boy next began to scream. His mother comforted him.

She felt like maybe she should have pressed the button for the Psychiatric Center, as she was half sure she was having a nervous breakdown. She stood totally perspiring, everyone else bundled into winter coats and scarves.

The sixth-floor door was already opening. In all the rush, she had forgotten to put on more lipstick. She fumbled in her bag, a hopeless enterprise, still half-looking for that contact lens as well. The not-to-be-located Revlon "stay-all-day" luscious coral lip gloss would help her regain some touch of color on the pale face she had seen in the mirror at the back of the elevator. She felt awful, really so terrible.

She flew into Room 609. She moved to sit on the edge of Michael's bed, hovering close to him for a moment but he slept deeply. His peaceful state allowed her to shift some, to angle herself toward the door, to cross and uncross her legs, not knowing who the next surprise visitor would be. For a moment she relaxed. Then Michael stirred. He roused. He took her hand and squeezed it really hard. He said, "I'm glad you're here Legs."

As he dozed off again, she thought the gray outside the window was a perfect reflection of her mood. And was that a run near the right knee of her new stockings?

How could she be a sex goddess with an unsightly run in her stocking? These black thigh-highs were guaranteed not to run. She'd purchased them at Neiman Marcus. These were not her run-of-the-mill Target stockings, the ones at the bottom of her drawer in her apartment for emergencies. Maybe the amnesia Michael was recovering from would distract him from such a sight. Would it be better for him to die and not see it? Knowing him, he would see it either way. Sometimes Michael was so tender caring and loving—other times so self-absorbed, unaware of anyone's feelings but his own.

She put her hand over the ghastly tear in her stocking, which made her look like she was falling into a yoga pose.

She tried to remember that she had a rather successful career. She had a real life outside of Michael. But she felt entirely unable to think of her small clothing business, imports and design, and how much she loved choosing the fabrics and working with the seamstresses. She was great in sales and now five major department stores carried her line. All that might be on the way to destruction, though, given that she hadn't been back to the workroom in two days, what with the urgency of guarding her territory. But she couldn't think of business. If she did, she would lose the work needed in this relationship. Remember, she was here to win. There was no room for any other campaign!

Why were the lights always so sharp, so *unforgiving,* in hospital rooms? Not even Angelina Jolie could look perfect in this horrendous glare. Everyone here had the same pallid green complexion. But then, didn't it follow that all Michael's ex-femme fatales would be subjected to this same ugliness? That gave her comfort. For a moment.

Honestly? *Waiting for Godot,* her favorite play, would be easier than this. At least with the play, one had a sense after the first hour that Godot would never arrive. The hospital guaranteed arrivals, women coming and going at any given moment. Wasn't Michael as desirable with one kidney as he was with two? Groggy, but still in control, he spoke slowly, coming up from his deep sleep.

"Hey Legs, be sure the nursing station doesn't send in more than one visitor? One at a time. Don't want more in the room." Did she count as one visitor? No time for mathematics.

Silently, she told herself, "You are special. Remember that." Her mind half-wandered to whether the hospital gift shop carried any sexy hose, before she told herself: "Remember. You are special."

Georganne stood up. She would act like she was delivering his message when in actual fact she was headed to the gift shop. After walking sideways out of the room to hide the run, she noticed a very attractive male visitor giving her the well-now-who-are-you look.

Couldn't this handsome stranger see that she was madly in love and all tied up? The only thing that was actually tied up was her stomach, but she reminded herself not to be negative. Success in her campaign was only two more wives and half-a-dozen girlfriends to overcome.

*

The gift shop smelled medicinal, the walls a cheerful shade of blue. A grey-haired woman behind the counter in an orange smock with a pin that said "Volunteer" smiled cheerfully while folding rubber sheets. "Can I help you, dear?"

The volunteer's smile was nothing but kindness, but that felt like nothing, given the other customers who were looking at Georganne, wondering why on earth she was wearing a Chanel suit and such high high heels. She was at a hospital, not a fashion show.

She decided to look only at the gray-haired woman. She mustered courage. "Do you have any stockings? I'm a medium."

"Of course, dear. I'll just step into the stock room. Back in a minute."

All that kindness and still, embarrassment flushed into Georganne. Desperation clouded her vision. She stepped back, suddenly slightly unsteady on her high heels, now bumping into the candy bar rack, knocking over the Mars Bars, peanuts and Hershey's. She tried to pick them up, just as Miss Volunteer returned.

"Here we are, dear. The very best after-surgery stockings anyone makes." She laid them out, thick, spongy, pale, beige, nothing like couture in Milan. "Is this what you have in mind?"

"Well. I—Not exactly. Do you have—Are there any other styles?"

The volunteer brightened. "No, but they come in black! But only in larger sizes. The patient is…recovering from what?"

"He's getting the—An arm prosthesis. For his arm." Again, she didn't know why she was lying. "So I don't think actually he'll be needing these. But thank you for your time."

Looking as if maybe Georganne were not, in fact, worthy of all the kindness, all the smiling, the volunteer stood waiting.

A hot flash came over Georganne, which she thought was the reason for the brilliant inspiration that made her ask, "Do you sell ballpoint pens? Or black magic markers?"

The volunteer brightened again. She produced a magic marker. "Certainly, dear. Is that all for today?"

"Oh thank you." But then Georganne saw the copy of last month's *Cosmopolitan* at the edge of the shop's actually quite ample magazine section. "The marker and this magazine." The cover seemed godsent: "HOW TO KEEP YOUR MAN THROUGH DIFFICULT TIMES."

Just as she felt the strong urge to tell the volunteer what she thought of volunteers: how wonderful they were, how much she admired them all—she remembered that anything and everything could be happening on the sixth floor. She needed to get moving.

Near the elevator, she sat on a bench for only the amount of time it took to color the skin on her leg that showed through the run with the magic marker. Hey…she wasn't just another pretty face after all. With a sense of power from having solved the disaster, she proceeded to the elevator button and took a deep breath.

*

She waited outside the room, until the floor nurse came by, to put the catheter in. Oh my, this was more work than any career move had been.

She stood trying to finish the article on "How to Handle the Unfaithful Male," but she decided he wasn't really being unfaithful. How unfaithful could he be in his post-op condition? She spent more time than expected, learning how to beat the odds on infidelity.

She was hurrying from the elevator, newly confident, when she saw a brunette walking toward the room with a big tray of croissants. They thought of everything on this floor for celebrities, so much better than the social worker last year who had come to Georganne's room just after her hysterectomy to ask did she want to talk to a priest or a rabbi? Now nauseous and upset at the memory of that social worker, she thought that a warm croissant would have served her better then talking to Buddha himself! Although, she would admit that there was something very seductive about the scent of incense and the way priests always seemed so very present.

She hastened toward Room 609, almost knocking into the croissant tray, when she noticed that the woman holding it was wearing Valentino. With Gucci pumps.

"Hello," Georganne said, lips dry and throat parched. "I'm Georganne."

In a beautiful French accent, she said, "Really? And I'm Michelle. You are one of Michael's relatives?"

Georganne thought: soon to be? A very *intimate* relative? But she shook her head softly and smiled. "No." Hoping to avoid more questions by asking her one, she said, "Are you a relative?"

"But not at all! I'm his girlfriend." She sounded so proud, so sure of herself. "He always loves the croissants I bake. I thought I'd bring him some. With his favorite jam. I know he may not yet be eating real food but the way I bake them, they last several days."

"Isn't that splendid?" Georganne wondered if she herself might last several days. Georganne's best culinary skill was choosing from the stack of take-out menus she kept in Michael's apartment. So, this croissant girlfriend was why she had to wipe off crumbs off his navy blazer on Thursday nights after he "visited his grandchildren"!

Narrowly, she managed to enter the room before Mademoiselle Croissants. "Michael dear. Your croissant girlfriend is here with her tray of goodies."

"You don't say. That's a great thing, Legs. I'd love you to meet her. Michelle. She's a fabulous baker. Has the greatest job at Sotheby's. Art appraiser."

Now. Michael was brilliant, but he didn't know a Jackson Pollock from a Matisse. Obviously art was not the main topic these two had discussed. Georganne assumed that this woman's art tended towards tactile sensory movement, very popular in the Moulin Rouge. "Georganne, you remember. I was born in France?"

She wanted to ask him: why didn't you stay there and save her from this crazy obsession with you? Meanwhile, she knew all too well that his foster home was middle-class Queens. It was baseball caps and McDonald's. Being born in France had no real effect on his current life except to impress Loulette.

Should Georganne bring up the French Revolution? Should she talk about how the last time she was in Paris with Michael she'd had flu and he'd asked her to spend her vacation at the home of her friend, because he'd be too busy to look after her?

Georganne had also been an art history major. Should she play the not-just-a-pretty-face game or discuss the rug that she and

Michael had just bought that looked like a Mondrian or should she do her sarcastic wit routine? She could always just sit quietly and listen like the good girl Michael liked to say she was.

When Michelle—of course she had the perfect feminine version of his name—did that gesture with her lovely brunette hair, Georganne understood she might not have won round one. This competition was something to take seriously.

"Art?" she said. "Do you like Mondrian?"

If looks could kill, she received a bullet through the heart from Michael.

As though Georganne had said nothing, Michelle asked, "How is Loulette? I heard she wasn't well, poor dear. Though she's in her late eighties, who can raise funds like Loulette? No one. Amazing efforts. She does it with such style and success."

"No one like her. And believe it or not, I'm ready to dig into of those great croissants. Georganne?" Now she was Georganne? Not Legs? "Legs" always seemed so demeaning from a man so successful, so well known, so well educated, so important in the politics of New York, but Georganne never told him what if felt like to be "Legs" instead of "darling" or "my love." He said, "Might you ask the nurse if she'd bring me a cup of tea? And…"—he waved a hand slowly through the air—"I think Michelle and I need a few moments to discuss the plans for this fund-raising event."

Georganne felt that funds weren't all that were rising, but like a good girl, she went to tell the nurse about his request for tea. She wished she'd been invited to stay. The brilliant way he had of putting together huge successful fundraisers was something she loved hearing. He was such a brilliant, creative and brave man, as shown by his army medals. She both loved him for all that—adored their interesting times together—and hated the way he sometimes treated her and perhaps all women. As she left the room she glanced at Michelle and thought "I'd like to hit you over the head with that silver tray and pour jam all over your Valentino suit."

When she had returned from asking the nurse for tea—the quickest errand of her life, full of terrible images of croissants and sticky sweet jam and catheters—she thought she would try to say something to get a conversation going: "Have you always liked to bake?"

Now this was shaky territory. Georganne hadn't even done well selling Girl Scout cookies. Her sweet tooth drove her closer to buying Double Oreos than baking French pastries. As much as she wished she could have told this French baker that she looked like a profiterole, Georganne had to admit, she was one good looking woman.

Her question met with only a quizzical look from the "girlfriend" and Michael leaning back into his pillows as if to take a small break from all of them. He had requested they be alone—as he had told her before, they had business to discuss.

Besides, her body was now busy expressing true feelings. She was dizzy. She needed to go somewhere else, sit down, she was feeling frail and had the urge both to close her eyes and to try to think of something entirely else like her business, her wonderful friends. Maybe it would feel good to count the squares on the floor? She reminded herself to breathe deeply, to force herself through the day, to pretend her thinking was all right. There in the hallway, on a small plastic love seat off by itself, she told herself that she was safe, that it was in fact a very good idea to take off her shoes. She didn't even realize that almost twenty peaceful minutes had gone by.

On top of all the mental and emotional distress, she had begun suffering from a bladder infection two days ago. It was really very painful. A blonde, a younger woman who must have been a dancer with a long, pretty ponytail, took a seat next to her. The woman's face was sweet but pale.

Georganne and the woman had shared smiles. They spoke of this and that about how difficult hospitals can be and about how convenient benches were when they appeared in hallways. Then the dancer said, "This is a funny thing to tell you. I mean. We just met. But I'm having a terrible time running to pee every other minute. I have the worst bladder infection."

Georganne couldn't believe her ears. "My—You won't—I'm in just the same fix!" She rummaged through her handbag and offered up one of her pills. "They'll make your pee orange, but not to worry. They help with the discomfort—and so very quickly."

All at once the nurse was before them saying that Michael had asked her to step out. She smiled in a most knowing and mysterious way before saying that his latest visitor had just left. He understood someone was waiting for him?

And to Georganne's dismay, she and the blonde stood up together.

"You're here to see Michael Sands?" the woman asked.

"Why yes I am," Georganne said. "Are you? You're…related?"

"Oh no. I'm his coffee shop pal. We meet some weekend mornings at the coffee shop on 9th when he goes out for his run. I guess you know him too. Funny, small world."

It really was funny, so funny that Georganne wished the pills she had just shared would turn the woman's hair and face as orange as her pee.

"You're his…" the blonde searched for some possible correct answer.

"Oh I'm a casual friend." More lies. She hoped. Though apparently things were getting more casual all the time.

Michael was propped up in bed eating a croissant and looking quite chipper for a man who'd just had surgery. He greeted Miss Weekend Morning Coffee with a big grin.

"Georganne," he said. "I'm glad you could spend so much time here today. I'm sure all my friends enjoyed meeting you"

Dizziness. She grabbed the bottle of Purell from the counter, not knowing whether to use it on her hands or to drink it or to hit Michael over the head.

Trying to contain her rage, she said, "I'm going out now." That would show him. That was how to be a good girl. "I'm sure I'll see you later."

Semi-embarrassed, the blonde murmured, "Oh, goodbye. Hope I'll see you again. Nice chatting with you."

Georganne walked down the corridor, one hand on the wall for support. At the entrance of the hospital she was greeted by a downpour. Her perfectly groomed hair would go entirely frizzy. She would be soaked, but she needed to breathe real air. She needed distance from the artificial lights, the TV sounds, the clatter of metal trays and the clatter in her head!! Breathing deeply, she walked around the sterile-feeling hospital streets.

But then, she understood that she needed to stop in before the night nurse came on and visiting hours were definitively over. Could her feet could take twenty more minutes in these miserable heels?

She told herself: she must remember that a strong woman stands her territory without drugs, hairdressers or the need for a second pair of stockings. As Michael always said, though she knew it wasn't his original phrase, "In life, one must always be prepared." He had accomplished several government missions with hugely successful results. He had no patience for one who was not totally prepared for all emergencies or for any person who needed tranquilizers to face danger. Especially if that danger was only the arrival of the next husband-hunting femme fatale.

She made it into his room minutes before the arrival of the night nurse, whose name she discovered just in time to feel that she had some small measure of control. "Darling," she said to Michael. "This is your night nurse, Shauna."

She was back to the role she'd landed in Act One, these now were the scenes where the Irish nurse failed in her attempts to seduce the patient, leaving the sophisticated goddess to take over the scene. Miss Night Nurse had beautiful seductive blue eyes, red curly hair and a lovely body.

Instead of letting on to any feelings of insecurity, she said, "Shauna do you like toffee?" She reached for the box on the nightstand to offer.

Michael seemed to have regained his usual demeanor In spite of quite a bit of discomfort, which she could see in his occasional grimace and how he moved a little gingerly. To the nurse he said, "Hey, honey, make yourself comfortable. You're going to be here all night. Or at least I certainly hope so." He then smiled at Georganne. "Night, Legs. Thank you for everything. Don't forget I love you. See you tomorrow."

*

She had to analyze why—with all the success she'd always had with men, with all her own accomplishments in fashion and theatre—why was Michael so important to her? Why would she even *want* to be his love. Why would she put up with him?

Believe it or not, when they were alone together he acted like the needy one. Their love life was like none she'd ever experienced. He was passionate but overwhelmingly lovely and his goal was to please her.

He had a lovely sister, and the nicest family and was happy to make them part of Georganne's life as well. Family was something she'd never known, coming from an icy background that left her with a huge need to feel part of someone else's family. With his sister, daughters and grandchildren, he always made sure Georganne belonged as well.

And taking his advice in business had led to even more success. He cared about her achievements.

Was all that worth the pain she felt at this need of his to prove himself to many other women—even if Georganne could almost see it as a game he played while he showed her love in so many good ways?

She walked along in what was only a light rain, feeling all the hurt and anger.

She would be calling her girlfriends again. For advice and to report on relationship progress or lack of it. To them she would look for comfort.

She was so *frustrated*—with him and with herself. Why was she part of this game? She hated sports. And she hated crying. Her mother always said that crying led to swollen eyes and her mother would know because her mother was always crying.

To distract herself, it was so much better to focus on the name of that actress who had played a nun. It seemed so important to remember. Even the name of the film! What was it? *Song of Bernadette? Ballad of the Sad Cafe?* Of course not! Those weren't even about nuns! Why was she thinking about this nun? Her thoughts were giving her a merry chase.

It was going to be a long empty night of images of candles flickering, nuns' habits open to the waist, background music. Maybe even a priest to marry them and, and, and… The silence, once the television was off, would be deafening.

It was Jennifer Jones!

*

The next morning she needed to go somewhere other than the hospital. She walked out into the street, shivering, but not knowing if she was hot or cold.

She was just thinking that maybe these four years of her life had been a downward spiral when a taxi pulled up and she had only to think—what a relief—of the moment. She climbed in without even knowing where she would tell the driver to go. Michael would be home in two days. He said that he really loved her. He had told her that she was handling everything so well, just as he knew she would.

"Rockefeller Center," said Georganne. She would get a table by the window, watch the ice skaters, order the best breakfast and their special latte. She was on thin ice. It might help her to watch people skate.

As she considered whether it would be eggs over easy or blueberry pancakes with tons of syrup and whipped cream on the side—she was truly at the end of her rope to ask for anything that caloric—she thought that the "game" was fixed. No one could win. And yet, still: no to pancakes and syrup.

The choices seemed to be: check into a mental ward, or check out altogether. Or pour drain cleaner into the bottled water in his apartment for that welcome home beverage!

The music and the warmth of the dining room made her doze for a moment. No one guessed—not even her—that she might be withdrawing, that she might be signing out of the game. In her half-dream fantasy, she wore a skating costume and had someone to skate with. As she half-watched skaters go round and round the rink, she wondered what their secret could possibly be. She thought: If I can't win, is this the first moment of a new life?

The music seemed to saying so. Some said it was the theme of her life: looking for love in all the wrong places.

Still, she felt destined to keep at this battle against Gilda, who wanted to be buried with Michael; also against the general wife in her commando boots and the croissant lady and the morning coffee blonde with the bladder infection. Even the Catholic Irish nurse with the gorgeous body. She was torn between conjuring up a new strategy or realizing this particular round of the game was hopeless. Maybe she must go somewhere where there was a chance of winning.

Everyone in the restaurant seemed to be looking at her. Or: it felt that way. She was the one who went to the hospital to see her lover's ex-wives and girlfriends wives, past and present. They all seemed to understand that she wasn't worried about Michael dying, just about his women and her ability to handle all this and still look and feel good enough to fight another day.

But watching the people skate on actual ice seemed to do her no good.

She paid the check. She climbed down subway steps, deciding to lose herself in the wintery late-afternoon rush. Another long evening lay ahead. She would end up alone, in her apartment with yet another can of soup and the sound of the telephone not ringing.

She had, in fact, focused so much on Michael that she wasn't really in touch with her many wonderful friends so much anymore.

Every single female on the subway could have told from miles away, that Georganne was anxious to get home to her man, a man who had sworn fidelity to her and meant it, though his promise was far from true. But she had forced herself to spend only two hours at the hospital the day before and how was she rewarded for her restraint this morning? A sign on the door read "NO VISITORS." The doctor said Michael needed to sleep, to be still and quiet in preparation for his release the next day.

*

She took yet another train. When she walked the four blocks from the subway home, it felt like forty miles. When she walked in, the doorman looked at her in what she thought was a sympathetic way so she forced a false smile and said, "Oscar! How have you been? Looks like snow, doesn't it?"

Moving toward the elevator, she almost fell over a large poodle bouncing out.

She turned the key in the lock. She took a deep breath as she turned on the light. How long had it been? All the plants on the windowsill had turned yellow. They hung limply from their pots. They were saying to her, "We feel as sad as you do!"

She threw her coat down and ran into the loud sound of silence and emptiness, to turn on the TV. It simply wouldn't do, to have her own voice feel like it was the only one in the room. Moving quickly through the voices of a weather forecast, she began to fill a pitcher for her poor plants when a new thought entered her head. She set the pitcher down on her small table. She understood that the game might be ending, but still, she found herself in front of the closet, looking to find a smashing outfit, just in case she was really needed at the hospital in a hurry. She had, after all, promised to help Michael arrange a car for the next morning and help get him back home. She might be losing this game, but she would finish her match with more than a little panache.

*

How could it be that the next morning was overcast and dreary? The day she was finally taking Michael back to their loft was gray? Inside their four walls there would be no more visiting wives and girlfriends. He would be all hers again!

The limousine—with Georganne in it—pulled up to the hospital door just as she had arranged. Standing there on the curb was a nurse, her back to Georganne, helping Michael up and out of the wheelchair. She could see how happy he was to be released, though his face showed a definite degree of pain.

She slid closer to the window as the car pulled up, hoping he could see her smile though the window just as the nurse turned, a hand on his elbow, and oh no! It was Miss Irish with the gorgeous body, her perfect breasts seeming even larger, even more shapely when, to Georganne's utter shock, she helped Michael into the car then settled *herself* on the seat on the far side of him.

Of course, there would be a private duty nurse to help him for the first days at home. Michael would need it. She had accepted that. But this nurse? The one now adjusting his seatbelt? This lovely creature would be in their home for a week.

"You remember Shauna, don't you Georganne darling?"

Her red hair looked newly coiffed and Georganne hoped she wouldn't succeed in reaching across to open the nurse's door and pushing her out before they reached the Village.

She had no idea what the three of them spoke of on the ride downtown. She could only recall silence. Her personality seemed to have disappeared entirely. She sat wondering when and where and how she could have lost it. Maybe she never had it. Maybe not at all!

Though as she sat, she did remember: regaling the group at a fundraising dinner with stories of her first marriage at age eighteen, living in Eagle Pass, Texas, the spinach capital of the United States, with its statue of Popeye in the center of town. She'd been the consummate New Yorker, even when she was told to "saddle up!" Everyone rode a horse. With western saddles no less. Indeed, she had known how to bring humor to every gathering.

"Georganne. Darling?" It seemed Michael had been trying to get her attention for more than a moment. "I know you want to take care of me every minute, but I wasn't sure that would be good for our relationship. Shauna will be perfect for the first week at least as I know you need time to work on your fall line."

Why. Why was she so insecure? So suspicious? Didn't he say she still had the best legs in this city of cities? Didn't he say that he had given me his greatest gift? The gift of making love? When they were alone, didn't he say how much he loved her? Didn't he help and support her business?

Her father had left the day she was born, her stepfather wasn't happy with her mother, so he focused his sexual desires on her. Compared to them, Michael gave her the world. He made her feel so complete. In comparison. His brilliance and humor and lovemaking made her feel a part of something, something she had always missed.

How could she only sometimes acknowledge to herself that he had a cold, cruel, womanizing side? Why was it so easy to forget when all she wanted was to belong to a man and a family.

In the elevator with the two of them, she was convinced there was a mechanical issue, but really she was the one shaking.

On the threshold, she said to Michael, "Welcome home, darling! I'm so glad you came through it the way we all knew you would."

He crossed to the couch and sat, with a happy but still fragile demeanor. "Come here, Legs."

He pulled her toward him while Nurse Shauna was getting set up.

"You know what, Beauty? I've been giving it a lot of thought. I'm happy to tell you: You've won. You've won over all my other ladies. You really know how to handle yourself with dignity. You never retreat into female weakness and antics. You know how much I hate that. You're my girl, Georganne. I'm proud to tell you that. Now I think I'll have a lie down for a while, then we can talk about the future. Ok beauty? That's a good girl."

*

After Michael had risen slowly and made his way into what Georganne had thought of as their bedroom of love and commitment, she found herself drifting toward the bookcase. There was a photo of her smiling on a boat in the Caribbean. There was the headshot from her modeling days. There was an image of her and Michael together. She took them and put them into the large handbag she had taken up from a nearby chair. She moved to the bar and collected her antique wine opener.

She moved into the bedroom.

Michael was lying on the bed on his back with his eyes closed. It almost looked like he was dead.

She opened the armoire, took out her sexy lingerie and added that to the bag.

It was difficult to look around and see what else she wanted because her eyes were filled with tears. He had given her family. He had made her feel proud to be hostess for all his important events, made her feel no one was more sexy or more fun to be with. Through all that she hadn't really seen the egotistical, cruel side that was surely a huge part of who he was.

By the front door she called, "Be back soon. Just going out for a few groceries." She didn't know if he or his nurse had heard.

It felt like years, waiting for the elevator to arrive. There were only six floors in the building. It was the slowest thing you could even begin to imagine. When the doors finally opened, Georganne gazed down into the small slice of space between the elevator car and the sixth floor where she stood waiting. She took the key to Michael's apartment, the key that had meant so much for so long, more than life itself. She dropped the key down the elevator shaft.

Goodbye key. Goodbye Michael. Goodbye to all the dreams and hopes this relationship had brought her!

The elevator door closed. No way, now, but down.

In the dim and gloomy space she tried to breathe. She couldn't see the numbers on the elevator panel because of her tears. She wiped her eyes. Now she could see "L" for lobby. The bag hanging from her shoulder was very heavy. She pushed "L" and turned her back on the panel so she wouldn't stop the elevator.

At the back of the small space, in the mirror, she saw a woman's face. It was drawn, tearstained, pale and unhappy. Georganne knew that woman. My God, she thought. That face was hers.

Suddenly, that face she stared into seemed to have a voice of its own.

The voice of the woman in the mirror, the woman she knew so well, that woman said to her, loud and clear, "Legs! Hey! Don't turn back! Just keep on moving."

TABLE FOR ONE

Of course, I could go to any restaurant now that Ronald left me for his bridge partner. I say to the maître d', "Table for one, please." Nothing to be ashamed of.

But a table in the middle of the restaurant? Why is everyone staring? Could they know Ronald? Know he left me? Maybe they could sense that not one time in my 89 years—not as a theater producer, the owner of a PR firm, co-founder of an empowering organization that promotes women in the film industry—have I dined in a restaurant alone.

The new hairdresser made my hair too bouffant and I look like my mother. Heavens. Anything but that.

At every single table: a couple. Only couples as far as the eye could see. Everyone would know that I alone, could not get a date. Not that I haven't had my share of exciting, loving dates. Six husbands. And counting? It's not that I need a man. It's that opening nights, sourcing trips to Europe, helping with acquisitions for the Aldrich Museum—all of that is so much more lively, so much more satisfying when *shared with a man*.

But no, I'll listen to my friends: I'll take out pad and pen and the whole place will think I'm finishing my novel for publication. Successful author is one title this nearly-ninety-year-old has not worn.

Meanwhile, in reality, I'll be jotting notes for what to say on Bumble, on Match, or OkCupid, as of course I'm looking for Ronald's replacement ASAP. My friend Bobbie is 78 and she found someone on-line, someone quite nice and elegant and who hasn't noticed she's from Queens. Soon, though, he'll have the sports channel on every night, certainly not the Broadway shows or concerts she envisioned. As for Bobbie, she might have somewhat large legs, but she wears stockings with seams up the back and takes care of herself and will almost certainly not go through life solo. "I will meet someone," Bobbie said. "I'm never finished with romance."

"Madame." Elegant waiter; tuxedo, lovely deep voice. "Can I get you a cocktail?" Then he said, "Dining alone?"

What kind of question is that? Hadn't he seen my writing pad and my lucky gold pen? Right before his very eyes I have become a well-known writer who does her best work in restaurants. I *choose* to do my best work in elegant restaurants. No one here could possibly have any idea about Ronald and how his bridge partner turned a card game into a full-time romance instead of a hand with no trumps.

"Soda water with cranberry and a slice of lime," she said. Always festive to look like a drinker, even if you're not one. Lift the pen, stay busy, think about how to start registering on the sites. What will get the quickest response? Of course, you'll use the sexy retouched photo from ten years ago, which is entirely fair because with a little Botox here and an eyelift there, you still look exactly like that.

"Sophisticated New Yorker wants to meet partner to share the cultural life of New York City and enjoy great intimacy." No, for heaven sake, it sounds like you're just looking to get laid. "Great intimacy" is the mistake here. "Intimate conversations?" What man can get through four minutes of intimate conversation without an attack of yawning?

Here comes the headache, hopefully not a migraine. And here comes the waiter, who so clearly senses my discomfort. I tell him I need a minute.

Maybe: "Loves romantic strolls by the Hudson at night." But what if it rains? Rain means horrendous hair. Kevin, husband number four, loved the Hudson, but would never take me on a river stroll. Instead, we gazed down at the water from our tenth-floor picture window. Safer to say, "Loves films, and concerts, not long walks." Kevin was a long time ago. Kevin was followed by John and Alan, husbands five and six, men I speak with often still, men I care for very much. Here I am in a restaurant, alone, unsure if I can sit through even soup, even a small green salad.

Here I am again, failing. The tendency is to judge myself, because growing up I was always expected to be perfect.

I sit up straighter in my elegant restaurant chair at my table for one, and I repeat the words my therapist has told me I must repeat: "Give yourself the grade of 100% for always taking the challenge. Even if you feel sad and rejected. You still deserve a gold star."

One blind date a couple of months ago, well before Ronald, was a man who told my friend Janet he wanted "a loyal companion." I can tell you he would have been happier with a cocker spaniel than a passionate woman like me.

Then, right in the center of this lovely restaurant, right here at 4th Street and Bleeker where everyone is in love, comes a hot flash. I'm taking double doses of my hormones to stay sexual, which is obviously not worth it at the moment. Maybe, "Loves a heated romance"? Too cute. And also, not cute at all.

If I add "Ninetieth birthday months away, but I look 50," it sounds like I spend all my time getting plastic surgery.

A friend's brother once called me for a date. He said, "Come chant with me?" Not even with a Valium could I comprehend three minutes of that. Dining alone is preferable.

Jay, my very first love—the first I can recall, from when I was very young—often took me to the Broadway Diner. We talked about books and the theatre. Jay, some called him Jazy, was shorter than me, but what did it matter. We only sat opposite each other at diner tables, never waltzing around a dance floor. Anyone who heard us laugh and saw us holding hands would have been jealous if they had never found a first love.

I would say, "Loves to travel" but I have learned that no man wants to spend day after day in Parisian flea markets or Milanese shopping arcades. What if he hears "travel" and drags me to churches or takes me on a sightseeing bus with people from Cleveland? He'll be the type who loves to eat from stands on the street and I'll get dysentery, which would kill the romance.

I would say "Romantic dinners" but if he's cheap he'll think that means eating in at my place, and who would want to move ahead romantically after seeing I use the microwave to store tax files? Elliot, husband number three, used to laugh at how cleverly I avoided being in the kitchen until he was entirely finished preparing gourmet cuisine.

Dinner tonight might be gourmet, but it won't be romantic.

I am far from Paris or Venice or the Winter Garden Theatre.

But I am also not sitting by myself in my kitchen. I am not alone in pajamas with cupcakes printed all over them watching television on a small counter-top set while feeding my naughty poodle under the table.

I am, in fact, in the center of a restaurant filled with couples in love. I have ordered a drink, yet to arrive. I have my pad of paper before me. I hold my gold pen, and notice a woman who is looking at the dashing man across the table from her in a way that might suggest that no amount of seduction will lift his rather sad smile.

Into my mind sails my morning horoscope: "Be on the alert to recognize your prime at whatever time of life it might occur." This. This might be my prime. Or maybe soon, maybe not tonight, but soon.

The waiter. Making his way over with a festive drink for me. He lowers it onto the white cloth tablecloth and smiles sadly, sympathetically.

I look up and I say, "Might I actually have the check? It seems I'm not hungry at all. Maybe next time."

THE BOY NEXT DOOR

There I was dressed in a hospital gown—ties in the back of course.

The procedure, not so serious, would temporarily relieve the back pain that had plagued me for months.

I can tell you: at 89 I know a thing or two about those white curtains that divide you from occupants on either side. There were three of us that morning, waiting for minor miracles.

Now, the *doctor*. He was cute. Very handsome. Brown hair. Wavy. More than a little like Gene Kelly with those bedroom eyes. He was asking me things like, "What medications do you take?" and, "Let's see, are you fasting?"

I wanted to ask *him* a few questions.

"Do I drink?" I echoed. "Oh no. Not for ages."

"Smoke?"

"Never."

When those baby blues looked up and he said, "No surgeries in the past six months?" I smiled, happy enough not to list the eyelift in 1991, the week at New York-Presbyterian for a facelift in 1999—though I did have the smarts to tell him of my gall-bladder removal and hysterectomy six years earlier. Of course, I confirmed my name was Georganne. I didn't list all the last names—too much to explain.

Dr. Dishy disappeared. On to the next victim. I could hear him on the other side of the curtain saying, "Your address is still 38 Mountain Ranch Road Santa Barbara?"

This fact was confirmed by a lovely deep voice that had me pushing myself up a little in my bed. Was there a hint of a British accent? I thought of the Santa Barbara foothills, the weekend reunion with the high school boyfriend who—after his failed marriage and 40 years living in Israel—whisked me off to San Ysidro Ranch. I still recalled the room service benedicts, our wood-burning fire. Back in LA he turned out to be quite boring—unless we were making love.

Through the curtain the doctor asked Mr. Potential, "Can you confirm your full name?"

He was Christopher. Penn. Aged Sixty-five. Six-foot-one and one hundred eighty-seven handsome-sounding pounds…and only a sheet between us.

"You're here today for"—rustling paper on the clipboard I would've given my eye teeth to rifle through—"an epidural steroid?"

"Sounds about right."

That *voice*. The two of us would glide through Montecito eucalyptus groves in his Astin Martin, a Grace Kelly scarf for me—minus the strangulation.

There had to be *something* unattractive about this man.

"I hurt my back," the voice told the doctor, "lifting a heavy canvas in my studio."

Oh my Lord.

Santa Barbara was almost two hours away from my Pilates. Three thousand miles from my beloved, native West Village. His Mountain Ranch was a world away from my hairdresser, my many doctors, my plastic surgeon, the only deli in all of California with decent corned beef. But he would love my warmth, my repartee. He'd appreciate my spirit of adventure and my joie de vivre so much that he won't mind relocating to my los-angeleno pied-à-terre.

What is love if not compromise?

And who would guess that after six husbands, after years of dating filmmakers who hadn't made a picture since 1948, writers without publishers, eighty-year-olds who were nine years my junior but couldn't muster the energy for a dance at the Carlyle or a walk in the rain—who could believe that my dream was on the other side of that curtain?

I was, of course, a fashion disaster. I had on a hospital-issue cloth shower cap, a paper gown starting to rip at the thigh and those atrocious blue sock-slippers.

But no time to dwell because on the other side of the curtain came another question: "Any other medical problems we should know about?"

"Can't think of a thing. Nothing important. Good general health, I guess."

The pain that hadn't let me walk or think for ages seemed almost beside the point. A dashing artist from Santa Barbara with ideal blood pressure, who never smoked or drank and who was young enough to remember his name without checking his hospital wristband was so close I could almost touch him.

"I try to work out four times week," he was then saying. "Though mostly I get exercise riding my horse."

I began to perspire. Though hospitals are ridiculously cold. I hadn't even put on foundation or mascara knowing, all too well, what a morning in the Surgery Center was like.

The plan: I would slip a note under the curtain!

But my bag and notebook were in the locker.

Imagine the laughs that Christopher Penn and I would have looking back on the irony of my meeting him, my ideal mate, my Mr. Forever, in the Pain Center.

I could always further his career by suggesting to our Board that we acquire his paintings for the New York office. We could auction a sculpture at the Irish Art Gala. Who wouldn't want a go-getter to help with his career the way I had with each of my husbands?

Later, in the Recovery Room, we would find ourselves near to one another, face-to-face, so to speak. He would be reading the Arts section—*New York* of course, an intellectual like Christopher would have no deep interest in L.A. papers.

"Any allergies?"

"None."

Oh, he will love my seafood casserole. All that basil, the creaminess.

My frustration was mounting. If my procedure was over first, I could hobble to the locker and pull on my clothes. I could apply the blush and eyeliner I never leave home without.

Worried that anesthesia would make me forget my own mission, I decided to make up a catchy name and say it over and over to myself: "The man behind the curtain"? Scratch that. Sounds like vaudeville, not the next man of my life.

But then the worst thing happened.

My name was called. I was being wheeled not down and to the left but right past him. Quick: the sheet up over my head.

The surgery room was cold—but the anesthesiologist was not!

He asked how I reacted to lidocaine, then novocaine. When I said I preferred Michael Caine he laughed real laughter. He said he loved my sense of humor. Of course, I made sure to be amusing, knowing by now that it was good practice to develop real affection with the doctor who was putting you under.

The room spun and before I knew it, I was in Recovery being asked if I'd like water, soda crackers, orange juice?

My dear friend Judy was beside my bed.

"Quick! Find Christopher!" I said.

"Who?"

"The perfect new man in my life! He's an artist…from Santa Barbara. Six-foot-one, 187. *Gorgeous.*"

Somehow, she knew exactly who I meant. She nodded. "Third bed from the door? Georganne. I'm sorry. He was just picked up. By a very handsome man. Oh, honey. When they left they were holding hands."

My heart sank in spite of the orange juice. One more dream smashed before it began.

But why on earth would I be blue? So many men, so many romances, so many starry evenings at the Met or drives up the coast—and so little time.

After all, the handsome anesthesiologist had liked my sense of humor. I needed to get his name. We women can't waste time brooding over a lost opportunity, now can we?

Driver's Seat

He cuts the engine of his "classic" pick-up and turns to me there on the bench seat. Looking into my eyes, he says, "I've finally found what I've been looking for all these years!"

He means…me? We've only known each other these few weeks! But at our ages—he's 76, I'm 89—it pays to move quickly. I do, after all, have lovely soft hands and good legs. I might be on the eve of ninety, but how many women of *any age* can say that in the past week they've ridden a horse, sold a valuable collage of her own making or were interviewed by their granddaughter, a sex therapist, on the crucial benefits of love making. What's so wrong, after all, with wanting to share my many pursuits and engagements with the right man? Could it be that my search on Match for "the one" might finally be over?

Though what if what he has "found after all these years" isn't me? Should I quietly swallow my jealous overwhelm? Should I say how happy I am for him? No. No.

Even now, voice quieter, he says, "I'm in love." He is saying to me, "Head over heels, Georganne."

"In love?" I echo.

"Yes! With a Bugatti!"

Now, he did go on to say vintage, which gave me a glimmer. I wished I could offer the overdrive an engine like that supplied. Maybe he views me as one of those BMWs from the sixties or seventies: good body, not such a smooth ride. Little does he know that husband number five never stopped saying how dynamite I was in bed. How to subtly let this new man know that a very intelligent gentleman from last year claimed that no woman had ever left his heart so broken? How to subtly let this one know that he will not fully appreciate me until he's tasted my fabled seafood salad. I'm a woman who always has candles in all the right places. He'll appreciate the effort—not to mention the floral nightgown and robe from Saks… roses become me. Romance? Always high on my agenda.

*

The next afternoon he picked me up, again in the pick-up, which was not exactly my speed, even if it is shiny and original, well-kempt and "one-of-a-kind." Apparently he's dying to visit a local auto showroom. "Just," he promises, "for a look around."

A showroom is far from a long wander through the Getty or making love late at night after Tosca at the Hollywood Bowl. But when this man and I are finally together, when any and all of my competition—of younger so-called actresses or heiresses—are in the rearview, I'll introduce him to my fun and festive dinner parties, to the pleasure of a wide blanket spread under that eucalyptus I love so much in Griffith Park.

Besides, after the showroom visit, we're heading to his urologist, the doctor who supplies the Viagra, the man I call Dr. Orgasm. Outside the office, I wait in the truck. I sit on the perfectly comfortable, if gauche, leather bench seat. I reach to place a hand on the polished walnut knob of the gearshift. I admire its embedded silver numbers.

My potential man emerges, waving the bottle like the winning ticket in a lottery.

Still, the way he occasionally lingers over his phone, the way he sometimes seems the slightest bit lost—not entirely uncommon at 76—makes me wonder if even my work-out classes and my twice-a-week yoga are not enough to bring real commitment. But he does, often, hold my hand while we drive.

He holds it even as I'm busy keeping my head down in case I spot any theatre friends as we drive by the Orpheum, the Palace, Grauman's Chinese. I tell him I'm looking for my phone, which I say is constantly lost—as lost as my social status would be if I were seen riding around the film capital of the world in an old pick-up.

He might own a vehicle that belongs on a farm but I'll tell you, there are moments when he gasps with what I know to be an admission of how much he cares for me.

Or there was that time he gifted me with a probiotic. All right, sure, not that romantic. But he had remembered—it was an opening night, not a good day for me to be unwell—how I'd said I needed to pick up a bottle. That gift of Gut Instinct meant he had been thinking of me.

*

All day, today, now, I've been waiting for a text, a phone call, a sign of togetherness. Last night was wine and pizza, and last night had lasted until this morning.

He sauntered out with a "Have a good day" that left me wondering if it was maybe a declaration of love. Then nothing. No calls. No texts.

Was he being cautious?

He will call me, soon. He will pen a letter and hand deliver it. He will arrive at the door with something warm and connecting and beautiful, maybe dahlias or an orchid.

After all, hadn't I arranged guitar lessons for him? Didn't I pick up his clothes from the cleaners that time? Don't I take his probiotics?

Meanwhile I haven't been the best at hiding my vulnerability. This might be a mistake.

But then, the next morning, his truck pulls up in front of the house. Through his rolled-down window—I move from where I had been staring at the street from *my* window—and I hear faintly as he calls, "Sweetheart!" while opening then slamming the door of his truck.

I open my door and he is saying, "See?" He leads me by the hand toward the street. "I was right! I've found it, Georganne. But should *it* be that Porsche I loved or the vintage Cadillac with the smooth ride?"

Really? More talk of cars? More about the pleasure to be had in falling for automobiles? I swallow disappointment. But disappointment that is beginning to turn into a smoldering anger. Is it always a car?

I told myself: Keep it under wraps. Act like you really don't care.

I miss my native, beloved West Village terribly. In this city of highways we are all always, always in cars.

Could this possibly be the afternoon when I begin to question my long-held conviction that one should never let her emotions show, given that one never knows what's coming next?

I hesitate at the sidewalk. He brightens, starts talking like he's been saving this piece of news all day. "I'm ready to introduce you, Georganne. I want you to really know who I am. To know what matters most in my life."

I squeeze his hand, thinking: family. Thinking: he wants me to meet his children; thinking: this right here is his old dead father's truck; his handsome brother rebuilt the thing. What could matter more in this life than family?

I catch my breath. My voice becomes just that much lower, just that much sexier. "You want to do what?"

"I want to take you on a camping trip."

I might be a slow learner. I might live my life in my own dream world. I might have married six men and I might have profiles on three dating sites. I am 89 years old and incurably romantic.

But I wake myself from this dream.

I let the man before me know that I won't be accompanying him. I consider the rehearsal schedule I'm due to review. I think of the meeting for the new acquisitions at the Aldrich that requires the reading of complex material.

I smile, in front of my house, and I say to him, "I won't be able to join you after all. I have far too much work to do."

MEETING BOB

I had just finished the launch of a hit show. *Night in November*. My partners and I had brought it from New York to Ireland. It opened on Broadway after a great run in Belfast's illustrious Lyric Theater. I had been high on the sellout success and only reluctantly returned to my pretty home in Beverly Hills. I had business there to attend. I lived alone—I was eighty-five at the time.

All through the plane ride I read the *Times* reviews. The play, *our* play, was "in many guises a plea for peace." The critics called it "fragile and magical."

Returning to any place, even a pretty one, after the *Times* called your work "fragile and magical," could seem empty. I had prepared myself. I knew it would feel bad. On the plane, newspaper in hand, I tried to think happily of the upcoming time in Los Angeles. But I knew that after three months in New York, nothing would ever feel as empty as California.

Obviously it was a Sunday, the loneliest day of the week, despite what Sinatra said about Saturday nights.

On this particular Los Angeles Sunday, I was minus a man in my life. This was a most unusual occurrence. Sinatra must never have experienced a Sunday alone in sprawling Los Angeles.

But then, there was the idea Monday. I was going to meet a man that a dear friend said I would adore. Honestly, though, her description sounded nothing like my type: pickup truck full of tools, very handy, can build anything I'd ever need. But! She also said he loved theater, cooking, music. She said an assortment of other interesting things. I trusted this friend. We had been close for decades.

The mere prospect of a new beau, maybe a new love match, made me so anxious that I'd chosen what to wear a week before. On the designated Monday, I sent my assistant out for a variety of sand-wiches and salads from my favorite deli. Who knew what this man would like to eat. Who knew if he would like me?

My outfit, "casual, nonchalant but still sexy," was laid on the bed. Still, I changed five times. I must have spent an hour on my makeup. I surely didn't want to seem like I was trying too hard but of course I wanted to wow him with my sexy style and my general appeal. You know, even some potential dud wearing overalls and a tool-belt required an effort. I nibbled on a Xanax to calm my nerves.

This was back in Nichols Canyon, that beautiful enclave in the Hollywood Hills where Suzy was a tenant in my guesthouse. Suzy had become very close with me, almost like a sister.

Casually, nonchalantly, on that Monday, Suzy looked up from sorting a pile of clothes and mentioned that she'd just seen an older man driving by the house. "More than once," she said. He'd slowed down at the property each time. Suzy was nocturnal and obsessed with all things true crime on television. She loved the Manson Family best, along with shows on assorted serial killers, though none of this went with her personality, which was sweet and funny.

When the potential overalls dud gentleman caller finally rang the bell, I opened the door.

This man on my step was so handsome! Even before he opened his mouth, I could tell he was warm and charming. I could barely believe my eyes. Not just that, but I could tell that he seemed impressed with me too. He came in. We talked and talked. About everything. After eating a sandwich with a cup of strong coffee, we adjourned downstairs to the terrace. I also wanted to show off some of my favorite artwork as I am a collage artist. Mr. Pickup Truck hap-pened to be an artist himself. This was beyond exciting.

Now, I had failed to mention to Suzy, as she was coming in and out with laundry, that I was planning to have company. She had gone out for the afternoon and left a load spinning. Soon she'd returned home to see, there in our driveway, the same truck that had been slowly passing by, again and again.

Suzy panicked. She *knew* the man had been casing the joint. He must have been a serial killer. At the very least Suzy was sure I had gone on match.com and—not knowing protocol and safety—I had invited a stranger right into the house.

She tried to enter from downstairs but the door was locked. She came in through the front door to find remnants of lunch on the table, but no one around.

Like a detective, she ran outside to the truck for forensic photographs. Then she really panicked. This truck was *immaculate*. Far too clean for anyone who wasn't a serial killer. Paralyzed by fear, she dialed 911. She explained the situation, a good looking older man had been casing the house all afternoon in an immaculate pickup truck and now that man had the owner of the home locked away some place where must've been robbing and torturing her. The police said Suzy should call back in a couple minutes if things hadn't changed. Never will Suzy nor I know why they didn't come right over. Maybe they'd had too many calls from Suzy in the past.

Meanwhile, downstairs, I was having the greatest first date of my life. The handsome older gentleman and I had so much in common. Yet we were so different. I was completely enamored of this brilliant person. So starry eyed, in fact, that I couldn't begin to hear Suzy calling my name and running around the house.

Finally, much later in the afternoon, our time together was coming to a close. I walked him to the door and out into the driveway when Suzy appeared from around the side of the house looking grave.

"Suzy!" I rushed to usher her over. "This is Bob. A mutual friend knew we had to meet. Bob drove all the way down from Northern California to meet me!"

Bob, in his typical warm manner, skipped the handshake and gave her a big hug.

"I believe I saw you outside this morning," he said. "I was making sure I had the right address. It's so confusing up in these hills."

As the color came back into her face in a relieved—or embarrassed—rush, Suzy said, "That makes perfect sense." Later she would laugh that for even one fraction of a second she thought Bob was even remotely evil.

*

To this day I don't think we've ever told Bob about all this. But it does make me laugh. The day I met the new love of my life, my closest friend almost had him arrested.

A SPECIAL INVITATION

She was in Hollywood because Martin, her latest husband, was now a big deal: Vice-president of a Major Hollywood Studio. He dragged her to Los Angeles kicking and screaming. It was, honestly, the loneliest place on the planet. She wasn't entirely sure of her feelings for him, but she disliked him more now that he was planning to disrupt her whole life. She had dropped all her New York plans.

Would anyone need an example of why her mild dislike of him was warranted? Who calls a city the size of Los Angeles "this town"? Martin does. But what does Martin know about anything, except making movies. Now, that's not really fair. He was a craftsman who constructed tree houses and the most fabulous kitchen chandeliers out of utensils, strainers, and pie cutters. He was so skilled. He was also a chef! And had so many other talents. The dislike, in fact, might have been her fears of giving up the only place she'd ever known.

Here was the thing: would she have the strength to make her own life in this desert? Maybe if she had a great project to work on. Maybe she needed to have an affair with anyone who wasn't a waiter-slash-actor!

*

She had never been one for joining clubs. Although, she was quite social. When first arriving at any party, she always wished she had stayed home. She felt shy. At least until she found someone easy to talk with. Then she might even be the life of the party.

Which was now a problem! When she was working in the theatre in New York there were so many parties. So many interesting people who were so easy to talk with. Life revolved, in exciting ways, around the current production. There was so much fun to be had with the cast and the other theatre people. It all was so familiar.

In California she was a stranger.

Being alone, she understood all too well, was the worst way of curing the loneliness. Being by herself presented overwhelming isolation, a dire need to be around others, and the conviction that she needed to start a new career. Eating too many chocolate bars, taking too many hot baths and calling her friends in New York might *seem* like the solution. But it wasn't working.

She wanted the friends she grew up with.

Also, she missed elevator attendant, a doorman to chat with daily. Living in California was the opposite of the congenial feelings she had walking into the apartment building each day where there were dogs and babies and other tenants who would say, "Looks like a hot one out there. Stay cool."

So. When a beautifully wrapped invitation arrived at their home with its thick cardstock and pretty lettering, all her psychotherapy raced through her brain. It was an invitation asking her to become a member of a Special Society. Could this be the solution? Already, everything about this felt good.

The mere word itself was so lovely: "society." This was not just a club. This sounded elegant. It rang bells in her mind that sounded very much to her like "Society of Debutantes," the one that had been so exclusive—not admitting her—at her alma mater, Finch Junior College.

Break the barrier, she thought to herself.

Take a chance for once.

Just *think* of joining.

Her one friend in this "town" was Allison. Allison was from Ohio. She was sometimes easy to be with. But sometimes she complained about the disaster of having to take care of her aging mother in a home called Happiness Villa out in the Valley. Her mother had lived there for five years. Her mother only had one child. But when Allison walked in the door and called out a cheerful, "Hello, Mom," her mother always yelled back, "Who's this?" Allison would understand if the trouble was Alzheimer's but it was extreme osteoporosis.

Still, Allison said she sometimes lapsed into thinking she was Paulette Goddard. Maybe, just maybe, if she'd been put in a home in Beverly Hills instead of Northridge, she'd be in a better state of mind.

"What do *you* think about my situation?" Allison asked.

Actually, she thought nothing of Allison's question. She was too involved with solving her social emptiness, too busy considering the possibilities of her new Society to think about someone else's weird mother.

After all, she still had to deal with Martin, who was now having three-hour lunches in the Warner Brothers commissary when in New York he always skipped lunch. What could that *mean*?

Martin had simply put their fabulous townhouse in the Village on the market and now he had little interest in anything but the size of his office and the "VICE PRESIDENT" on the door.

She had never expected that moving West would mean he'd fall more in love with her, and he didn't. But she also didn't expect that he would now lavishing all his love on any item of clothing marked RALPH LAUREN, on the very newest, most expensive red convertibles, on being able to get the best table at Spago's at a moment's notice.

There on the invitation were words that gave this new Society a sea-side air. It actually sounded nautical.

She loved the ocean and loved even the thought of what she might wear for that chic yacht-club look. Her new sailor slacks with a navy-and-white striped shirt? That new hat with the navy brim! She loved the salt smell of getting close to the ocean.

Was her psychotherapy working? Thoughts of this new society were not driving her to run for safe shelter.

Instead, with a blind leap, she rushed to the phone. She would call them. Immediately, she was connected with a man's voice, deep southern accent. He asked where she lived, as he had several stops in her neighborhood. He could come by soon. Imagine!

And suddenly the room grew hotter. She was hot and cold at the same time. But also, excitement began to take over.

While waiting, she listened on the phone to Allison. Allison spoke on and on about cooking and how her three-year-old was wetting the bed. These were things she knew nothing about. When she returned to the table, there was no reason to turn the conversation to the gallery she missed so much on Park and 56th or to which show was opening that week on Broadway. But she had to talk to someone about something so she talked with Allison.

They spoke of the protein diet. Who in this City of Angels wasn't trying to lose weight?

Maybe that's why dealing with social encounters, especially with people not from New York, brought about a need for an emergency call to her therapist.

When would he arrive? The man she now thought of as the "main man" in the Society that would save her from the emptiness of this desert?

She would never, never, talk to Allison about this sudden need to join. No one would understand because being married to a Hollywood producer sounded exciting to the average person. But it wasn't always wonderful, and often quite lonely.

Finally! Now! the bell!

She opened the door. On the step was an elderly gentleman. Could he be wearing…a trucker's cap? One that said St. Louis Rams? This did not strike her as very nautical.

There was, in fact, nothing nautical about him. His overly bright plaid shirt matched the huge smile that exposed a set of the whitest false teeth. She could tell they were false because when he smiled, they made a crackling noise.

Urgently, from the porch, before even entering, he said, "You don't mind if I use the facilities?"

She guessed that was safe?

But the old anxiety was starting up. Pushing into her home, her safe shelter, was a new person to contend with. She couldn't hang up. Or even run away.

Returned from the facilities, he sneezed. He coughed. He began to tell her not to be bothered by his allergies. The doctors hadn't been able to find out what he was allergic to. He coughed. He blew his nose. He thought it might be cleaning solution, but before he had a chance to list further possibilities, she asked, "So, about this Society of yours?"

He—this new friend—was suddenly interested as well. He pulled out a chair at the dining room table. "I'm Thomas. Some people call me Tom. I prefer Thomas."

She had never so much as dated a "Tom." It sounded more Midwestern than a name you'd encounter at a Fifth Avenue dinner party. "Thomas" might actually work here. She told herself to start things off in a positive way.

"All right, Thomas. What is this Society all about?"

He cleared his throat, coughed. He blew his nose loudly into a tissue he then tucked into the pocket of his khaki slacks. Finally, he opened a briefcase and a folder embossed with gold. It was a thing of beauty.

"Is this"—he leaned closer, seeming deeply interested, almost concerned—"for yourself? Or is it for your husband?"

The question seemed odd. Why would I speak to him about a membership for Martin? "Well, of course it's for me."

"So, it's you who's choosing to be cremated?"

"*Choosing what?*"

"Oh we'll get to the choices. This is one of the most caring gestures you can offer to loved ones. The Neptune Society is America's most trusted cremation service." From the folder he opened and pulled out what looked like two credit cards. "These cards right here are so convenient."

"But I—"

"Fits right into your wallet. Or your husband's if you offer this same service to him, which is a very compassionate gesture. Anything happens to him, all the information is immediately available. Phone numbers. Right there. He'll want to carry this card with him at all times."

"But for Martin I—"

He interrupted, voice low, "Does his death seem imminent?"

Entirely unsure how to get him to stop talking, let alone out of the house, she found herself asking, "Would you care for some grapes?"

"Mrs. Bancroft, I don't think you're giving yourself enough credit for the importance of this arrangement."

"No, you see, I—"

"This is an investment in peace of mind. A gift for your beloved's future."

Now. This last word, it hit home. Her beloved's *future.*

The fact was, Martin might be newly vice-president of a major studio, but he wasn't getting any younger. He was even older than she was. Maybe what Martin was really searching for, out here in the land of youth—even if he himself didn't know it—was actually, in fact, *peace of mind.* Maybe, in addition to a three-picture deal, he would be fulfilled with a constant reminder of the knowledge that his future was settled—sunny even—with this new card in his wallet. Deep down he would understand that it wasn't as morbid as it sounded. He would see that she really did have his best interest in mind. What did he have, another ten really *good* years? In the meantime, he could claim membership to a great international organization. He would achieve a membership he would never need to cancel.

She imagined sneaking the card into his wallet. It would slip in right behind the new card she'd discovered last week when look-ing through his things for clues to any outside life in this strange place. Her husband had become, the glossy black card told her, a full-fledged member of *Sexy Lingerie* on La Cienega. But he hadn't yet replaced his white boxer shorts for floral ones. More importantly, there was no brand-new slip or negligee in her closet. What exactly did that membership offer?

But there was more pressing business at hand, she reminded her-self as Thomas cleared his throat. Only consider the present moment.

But honestly, Ralph Lauren? She would give him Ralph Lauren. *Sexy Lingerie?* This boldness! This sexy card right in his wallet! Why on earth had he dragged her out to this coast where she felt so alone? He'd be cremated all right. In two of Ralph's jackets, not one. Suddenly she wanted nothing more than to watch those tiny signa-ture polo ponies go up in smoke.

But she loved Martin. Maybe thoughts of his possible death would shock him into the idea of a monthly long weekend holiday together in New York. Maybe forcing him to carry a card that made cremation seem imminent would make him want to spend quality time with her.

"Did I say something funny?" said Mr. Tom. "Is it this great installment deal? Especially tailored to your needs. Monthly payments automatically deducted from your bank account."

"*My* account? I'm sorry. I have decided, after all, that a membership would be a perfect gift for my husband. Feel free to deduct from our joint account."

She would no longer need those beautiful new sailor-motif pants, no excuse for the striped boat-neck shirt. What was fitting for a memorial service following a cremation? Apparel that says, "I am sad. But I'm also quite available."

She would miss Martin. They'd had some beautiful times together. He was kind and loving. But one never knows. He might get crushed by a toppling studio set. And wasn't his next picture shooting in Kenya? There he could be stepped on by an elephant! At least one aspect of his future would be entirely knowable and he would carry a card to prove it.

Her thoughts turned back to cremation wardrobe: Not black in Hollywood. Navy? With her beautiful jade necklace. Definitely a short skirt. Not heels, but not flats either. Great legs would surely be the turning point.

Because there would, of course, be single and widowed men attending. She would be more than happy to step in, to take on her newest role: "Widow of the Neptune Society."

WHERE HAS THE MUSIC GONE?

"I'd like to start again with you. Can I play you that song? The one I wrote for especially for you?"

This was Norman, my partner for thirty-six years. I had walked into his apartment overlooking the Hudson and found him sitting at the piano.

"Of course." I tried to hold back the tears. What a sweet, funny, still-sexy man this was that I spent much of my life with.

I kept having to remind myself that we were, in fact, still married though I hadn't seen him in weeks and weeks. Maybe years. I had never attempted to separate legally.

I had simply started a new life.

It has been five years with lovely, caretaking Bob who the gods brought to me even when I was still with the Norman I knew and loved. Back then, five years before, Norman was going further away each day and always angry at me.

Little did I know when our life together was getting sadder and more strange feeling, that the Alzheimer's had begun. It was disease that turned him into this frustrated man, constantly displeased at everything I did, always so angry.

We had worked together often in our many years together.

He and his writing partner did all the music and lyrics of the musicals we produced. I handled sales, contacts. I was used to beautiful sounds coming from our living room, melodies and refrains accompanied by Mel's haunting voice. We were such a beautifully matched threesome. Each of us did what we did best. We traveled together presenting our shows to producers, meeting with backers. The house of our Hamptons summers had a separate music room. I would float in the pool, listening to the notes floating in the air. I swam. Norman composed.

Today, the piano bench in my living room sits empty. I want to smash all the keys and wreck the dark wood and all the memories it holds. Its silence fills the room. Sometimes sitting alone in that room, I still hear the sounds of the songs being sung over and over until Norman cried, "Now! No we have it. That's it. The song's complete." Then he would call out to me, "Come and listen."

Where is the music now? Forever in my head? Sometimes in my dreams.

I hadn't seen Norman often in the past year as flying had become risky. There I was, eighty-nine years old in Beverly Hills. He in New York with a caretaker and his son two blocks away near his favorite, Zabars, on the corner.

Together with my new, loving Bob, I had fixed up Norman's new apartment in the part of the city he loved best. He kept telling me last night that this little apartment was his all-time favorite. It made me joyous to know that.

But the good feeling couldn't overcome the sadness.

With all his medications, Norman's not angry anymore. He's not frustrated. He's calm and sweet. He's never been so glad to see me.

But did he remember any of those feelings after I left? I hoped so. But I also hoped not. Just thinking of it, I'm overwhelmed with guilt. I should have stayed with him. But how could I? I, who need help in certain ways managing myself at this advanced age. I could never have handled the situation alone.

"Can I play you another song?" he asked now, here in the living room of the apartment he said he liked so much.

"Of course," I said.

"It's one I just wrote. You'll like it." It was a song he taught Kirk Douglas to sing decades ago in London while creating *Jekyll and Hyde* for television. It was called "Great Expectations."

He began to sing: "I had such great expectations tomorrow would never come."

I tried to hold back the tears. I had such great expectations. I thought we'd always be together. I had to face that our tomorrow would never come.